W9-BRI-631

# Math Practice

## Reinforce and Master

## Basic Math Skills

### Grades 5–6

---

**Credits**

**Author:** Bill Linderman

**Production:** Quack & Company, Inc.

**Illustrations:** Michael L. Denman

**Cover Design:** Peggy Jackson

**Cover Credits:** Photo www.comstock.com

© 1999 EyeWire, Inc. All rights reserved.

---

          ISBN 0-88724-938-8

# Table of Contents

## Numbers and Operations

## Fractions and Decimals

## Multiplication and Division

## Algebra

## Review

## Geometry

## Measurement

## Data Analysis and Probability

## Review

## Introduction

*Math Practice* is filled with fun and challenging activities to help students develop and review a wide selection of math skills. Students will practice adding, subtracting, multiplying, and dividing whole numbers and fractions; learn basic algebra concepts; explore data analysis and probability; and much more. Easy-to-follow teaching elements accompany many of the skills. These elements will help build a mathematical foundation for the students. Review units are included midway and at the end of the book. These units assess the skills practiced. Teachers and parents will find *Math Practice* a valuable tool for helping students achieve growth in their mathematical development.

Name _____

# Speak in Numbers

A number, such as 1,234, can be written in several ways.   **standard form** = 1,234
**word name** = one thousand, two hundred forty-four   **expanded form** = (1,000 + 200 + 30 + 4)
   $5\frac{1}{5}$ = five and one-fifth      3.5 = three and five-tenths      -8 = negative eight
                                    or three point five

Write the word name for each number.

A. 3,187 _____

B. 21,067 _____

C. 427 _____

D. 1,800,234 _____

Write each number in expanded form.

E. 456 _____

F. 43,567 _____

G. 234,678 _____

Write each word name in standard form.

H. eight thousand, four hundred forty-three _____

I. forty and one-sixth _____

J. negative six _____

Complete the puzzle.

**Across**
4. -2
7. 0.2

**Down**
1. $\frac{5}{10}$
2. -4
3. 42
5. $\frac{2}{3}$
6. 2.1

Name _____

# Digit Detective

| billions | | | millions | | | thousands | | | ones | | |
|---|---|---|---|---|---|---|---|---|---|---|---|
| hundreds | tens | ones | hundreds | tens | ones | hundreds | tens | ones | hundreds | tens | ones |
| 3 | 6 | 4 | 1 | 9 | 0 | 2 | 4 | 6 | 2 | 0 | 6 |

Write the value of each underlined digit.

A. 234,415 _____

B. 1,234,567 _____

C. 4,567,879 _____

D. 779,132,354 _____

E. 556,132,453 _____

F. 9,768,453,657 _____

Follow the directions using the number below.

# 3 1 5 , 6 0 9 , 2 5 4 , 5 4 6

G. Draw a box around the digit in the one hundred billions place and the ones place.

H. Draw a circle around the digit in the one hundred millions place and the one thousands place.

I. Draw an arch on top connecting the square in the one hundred billions place and the circle in the one hundred millions place.

J. Draw an arch on top connecting the circle in the one thousands place and the box in the ones place.

K. Draw a triangle between the digits in the one millions place and the one hundred thousands place.

L. Draw an arch on top connecting the digit in the one millions place and the digit in the one hundred thousands place.

M. Draw an arch underneath connecting the circles in the one hundred millions place and the one thousands place.

Name _____

# Read and Solve

Find each sum or difference.

A. David found out that there were 3,482 fifth and sixth graders in his school district. His best friend, Sam, lives in a school district that has 3,288 fifth and sixth graders. How many more students does David's school district have?

B. Cheryl just found out that there are 252,000 people living in Schnocklesville, where she was born. Flipperflop, where she resides now, has a population of 832,000 people. Which town has a greater population? What is the difference?

C. This year, 845 fifth graders and 964 sixth graders from our district visited the Science Museum. Along with these two groups, 539 fourth graders made this their choice of field trip destinations. How many students in all from our district visited the museum?

D. Marco had a blast talking to the cafeteria manager yesterday. He found out that last year the students at our school drank 84,290 pints of milk. Can you imagine that? And to top that off, 61,249 slices of pizzas were served to our school's hungry, growing students! What was served more last year, milk or pizza? How much more was served?

E. Skate shoes are becoming very popular at Gwen's school, Lakeside Elementary. There are 98 students that flip out their wheels to get from point "A" to point "B." The Skate Store at the mall has sold 2,472 pairs of these fancy forms of transportation! If all of the skate shoes from Gwen's school were purchased at The Skate Store, how many skates are being used at other places?

F. At the ballpark, 29,359 hot dogs and 9,244 pretzels were sold. How many hot dogs and pretzels were sold?

Name _____

# Time to Order

When comparing numbers, remember these rules:

1. First, compare numbers by comparing their whole number parts. The larger the number, the greater the value. If the whole numbers are the same, compare their decimal parts or fraction parts. If numbers are negative, the value of the greater digit is less.

$$82 > 24 \qquad 5\frac{1}{4} > 2\frac{1}{4} \qquad 3\frac{5}{6} > 3\frac{1}{6} \qquad -10 < -7$$

2. When comparing decimal parts, the closer a digit is to the decimal point, the greater its value.

$$0.5 > 0.05 \qquad\qquad 0.0043 > 0.00043$$

3. When comparing the fraction parts, change to equivalent fractions having the same denominator.

$$\frac{1}{3} \bigcirc \frac{4}{12} \qquad \frac{1}{3} = \frac{4}{12} \qquad \frac{4}{12} = \frac{4}{12} \qquad \frac{1}{3} = \frac{4}{12}$$

4. When the numerators of fractions are the same, compare the denominators. The smaller the digit, the greater its value. $\qquad \frac{2}{5} > \frac{2}{7}$

Order each from least to greatest.

A. 2,345; 5,432; 3,245; 4,324 _____ _____ _____ _____

B. 42,006; 4,237; 456,123; 43 _____ _____ _____ _____

C. 3; 45,007; 2,404; 435,132 _____ _____ _____ _____

D. $\frac{1}{3}$ , $\frac{1}{6}$ _____ _____

E. $\frac{3}{5}$ , $\frac{2}{10}$ _____ _____

F. $\frac{1}{3}$ , $\frac{1}{4}$ _____ _____

G. -4; -7; -9; -10 _____ _____ _____ _____

H. 3.6; 3.2; 6.4; 6.9 _____ _____ _____ _____

I. 0.02; 0.2; 0.0002; 0.002 _____ _____ _____ _____

 Order these numbers from greatest to least: 3.2; 0.032; 3.0032; 33.332; 0.332

_____ _____ _____ _____ _____

Name _____

# The Big Sale!

Follow these steps to find the percent of a number.

Example: 30% of 65

First, write the percent as a fraction. $30\% = \frac{30}{100}$

Then, convert the fraction to a decimal. $\frac{30}{100} = 0.30$

Multiply by the decimal.

30% of 65 = 19.50

$$\begin{array}{r} 65 \\ \times\ 0.30 \\ \hline 00 \\ 1950 \\ \hline 19.50 \end{array}$$

Write the percent of each number.

A. 30% of 25 = _____     25% of 40 = _____     1% of 30 = _____

B. 50% of 484 = _____     10% of 35 = _____     20% of 95 = _____

C. 5% of 80 = _____     20% of 45 = _____     10% of 500 = _____

D. 15% of 42 = _____     80% of 15 = _____     25% of 50 = _____

The big sale! Find the percent saved. Subtract. Then, write the new price.

E.

Original price: _____

Amount reduced: _____

Sale price: _____

F.
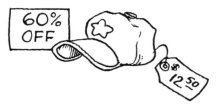

Original price: _____

Amount reduced: _____

Sale price: _____

G.

Original price: _____

Amount reduced: _____

Sale price: _____

H.

Original price: _____

Amount reduced: _____

Sale price: _____

Name _____

# Packed Full of Power

Numbers can be abbreviated using exponential and scientific notation.

An **exponent** tells how many times a factor is multiplied by itself.

$5^3 = 5 \times 5 \times 5 = 125$      5 is multiplied by itself 3 times.

**Scientific notation** is the power of 10 multiplied by another number between 1 and 9.

$7,000,000 = 7 \times 10^6$

Hint: To know what power of 10 to use, simply match the power of 10 to the number of zeros in the number.

$4,\underline{000} = 4 \times 10^3$        $9\underline{00,000} = 9 \times 10^5$

Write each number using an exponent.

A. 3 to the fourth power _____

B. 6 to the third power _____

C. 9 to the eighth power _____

Solve.

D. $2^3 =$ _____         $6^2 =$ _____         $4^4 =$ _____         $7^3 =$ _____

E. $3^2 =$ _____         $1^{10} =$ _____         $3^4 =$ _____         $9^2 =$ _____

F. $4^3 =$ _____         $2^5 =$ _____         $0^4 =$ _____         $3^3 =$ _____

Write the value.

Clue: $10^1 = 10$, $10^2 = 100$, $10^3 = 1,000$, $10^4 = 10,000$, $10^5 = 100,000$, $10^6 = 1,000,000$

G. $3 \times 10^2 =$ _____         $8 \times 10^3 =$ _____         $6 \times 10^6 =$ _____

H. $6 \times 10^4 =$ _____         $4 \times 10^5 =$ _____         $5 \times 10^2 =$ _____

Write each number using scientific notation.

I. $7,000 =$ _____         $5,000 =$ _____         $600,000 =$ _____

J. $8,000,000 =$ _____         $40,000 =$ _____         $3,000,000,000 =$ _____

Name _____

# Factor It Out

A **prime number** is any whole number that has only two factors, itself and 1.

5 is a prime number. It has only two factors: 5 and 1.   5 x 1 = 5

Any number that is not a prime number is a **composite number**. **Prime factorization** is finding the prime factors of a number. A factor tree can be used to find the prime factors.

To find the prime factors of 24, start with any two factors that equal 24.

The prime factors of 24 are 3, 2, 2, and 2.

24 = 3 x 2 x 2 x 2

Use a factor tree to find the prime factors for each number.

A.        28              21              16              48

B.        36              40              32              24

C.        15              18              20              50

D.        27              30              55              42

Name _____

# Pizza Delivery

**Fraction of a whole:**
2 pieces are missing.
Fraction of pizza left = $\frac{4}{6}$

**Part of a Set:**

How many marbles are shaded? 3

How many marbles are there altogether? 5

What fraction of the marbles is shaded? $\frac{3}{5}$

**Location on a number line:** $\frac{4}{6}$ =

Write the fraction for the shaded part of each picture. Reduce to lowest terms.

A.   B. 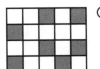  C.   D.   E.   F.

Shade the fraction listed.

G.   H.   I.   J.   K. 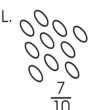  L. 

$\frac{2}{5}$   $\frac{5}{8}$   $\frac{1}{3}$   $\frac{7}{8}$   $\frac{6}{7}$   $\frac{7}{10}$

Identify the fraction.

M. 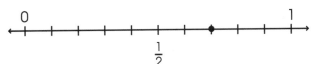  N.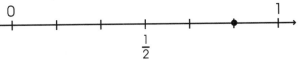
$\frac{1}{2}$   $\frac{1}{2}$

O. 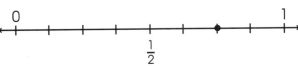  P. 
$\frac{1}{2}$   $\frac{1}{2}$

Name _____

# A Quick Change

A fraction can be converted to a decimal using division.
Divide the denominator into the numerator.
The quotient becomes the decimal.

$\frac{1}{4}$

$$4\overline{)1.00}$$
$$\begin{array}{r} 0.25 \\ 4\overline{)1.00} \\ -8 \\ \hline 20 \\ -20 \\ \hline 0 \end{array}$$

$\frac{1}{4} = 0.25$

Convert each fraction to a decimal.

A. $\frac{3}{6}$ = _____     $\frac{4}{10}$ = _____     $\frac{1}{10}$ = _____     $\frac{2}{20}$ = _____

B. $\frac{1}{5}$ = _____     $\frac{2}{8}$ = _____     $\frac{1}{20}$ = _____     $\frac{3}{4}$ = _____

Convert each fraction to a decimal. Then, write the pattern on the line below.

C. $\frac{5}{10}$ = _____

$\frac{4}{8}$ = _____

$\frac{8}{16}$ = _____

_____

D. $\frac{1}{5}$ = _____

$\frac{2}{5}$ = _____

$\frac{3}{5}$ = _____

_____

E. $\frac{1}{4}$ = _____

$\frac{2}{4}$ = _____

$\frac{3}{4}$ = _____

_____

F. $\frac{8}{16}$ = _____

$\frac{4}{5}$ = _____

$\frac{2}{3}$ = _____

_____

$\frac{1}{8}$ = _____

$\frac{3}{8}$ = _____

$\frac{5}{8}$ = _____

$\frac{7}{8}$ = _____

_____

Name _____

# A Wacky Web

**Percent** means parts of a hundred. A decimal can be converted to a percent by changing the decimal to hundredths.

$40\% = \frac{40}{100}$        $40\% = \frac{4}{10}$        $4\% = \frac{4}{100}$        $4\% = \frac{40}{1000}$

$40\% = 0.4$                $4\% = 0.04$

Convert each decimal to a percent.

A. 0.6 = _____     0.1 = _____     0.75 = _____     0.9 = _____

B. 0.25 = _____     0.06 = _____     0.28 = _____     0.15 = _____

C. 0.8 = _____     0.5 = _____     0.35 = _____     0.4 = _____

Draw a straight line to each matching set of decimals and percents.

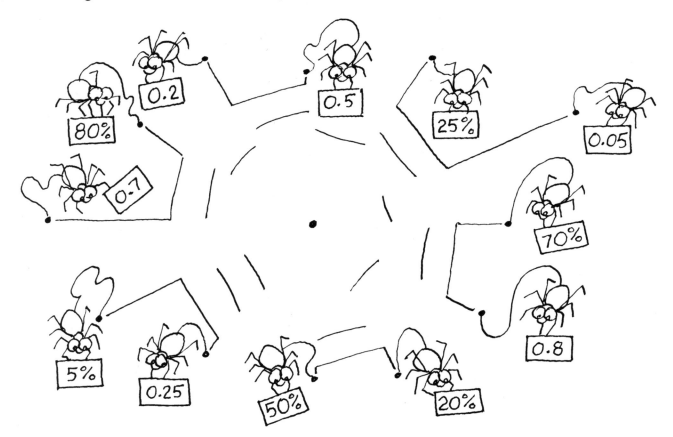

Name _____

# Triplets

There are three ways to write the amount for the picture.

1. Write the fraction.

$\frac{1}{2}$

2. Divide the denominator into the numerator. Write the decimal.

$$2\overline{)\begin{array}{r} 0.5 \\ 1.0 \\ -1.0 \\ \hline 0 \end{array}}$$

3. Write the percent.

$\frac{5}{10}$ = **50%**

Using the Number Box, write the decimal and percent for each fraction.

A. fraction: $\frac{1}{4}$

decimal: _____

percent: _____

B. fraction: $\frac{3}{4}$

decimal: _____

percent: _____

C. fraction: $\frac{1}{10}$

decimal: _____

percent: _____

D. fraction: $\frac{1}{2}$

decimal: _____

percent: _____

E. fraction: $\frac{1}{5}$

decimal: _____

percent: _____

F. fraction: $\frac{1}{8}$

decimal: _____

percent: _____

### Number Box

| | | |
|---|---|---|
| 0.125 | 20% | 80% |
| 25% | 0.8 | 0.25 |
| 12.5% | 5% | 75% |
| 0.1 | 50% | 0.2 |
| 0.5 | 0.75 | 10% |
| 0.05 | | |

G. fraction: $\frac{1}{20}$

decimal: _____

percent: _____

H. fraction: $\frac{4}{5}$

decimal: _____

percent: _____

Name _____

# The Common Link

The **least common multiple** (LCM) of any two numbers is the smallest multiple that is common to both numbers (other than 0).

| The first six multiples of 3: | | The first six multiples of 4: | |
|---|---|---|---|
| 3 x 0 = 0 | 3 x 3 = 9 | 4 x 0 = 0 | 4 x 3 = 12 |
| 3 x 1 = 3 | 3 x 4 = 12 | 4 x 1 = 4 | 4 x 4 = 16 |
| 3 x 2 = 6 | 3 x 5 = 15 | 4 x 2 = 8 | 4 x 5 = 20 |

multiples of 3 = 0, 3, 6, 9, 12, 15 . . .          multiples of 4 = 0, 4, 8, 12, 16, 20 . . .

The number 12 is the least common multiple (LCM) of both numbers.

Find the least common multiple (LCM) for each set of numbers.

| A. 2, 3 | 2, 9 | 3, 9 | 2, 8 | 5, 6 |
|---|---|---|---|---|
| B. 4, 5 | 2, 4 | 4, 8 | 6, 8 | 8, 9 |
| C. 3, 5 | 3, 6 | 2, 6 | 4, 6 | 2, 10 |
| D. 2, 5 | 6, 7 | 5, 10 | 7, 14 | 3, 12 |
| E. 3, 7 | 4, 9 | 2, 7 | 3, 10 | 5, 15 |
| F. 3, 8 | 5, 9 | 8, 10 | 4, 12 | 6, 12 |

Finding the least common multiple is a great way to find a common denominator when adding or subtracting fractions.

# The Greatest Common Factor

The **greatest common factor (GCF)** of two or more numbers is the greatest number that is a factor of each number. To find the GCF of a pair of numbers, list the factors of the numbers.

8 = | 1  2 | 4  8
10 = | 1  2 | 5  10

The common factors are 1 and 2. The greatest common factor (GCF) is 2.

Find the greatest common factor (GCF) for each set of numbers.

A.   3, 9 _____        7, 14 _____        5, 40 _____

B.   4, 12 _____       9, 18 _____        10, 20 _____

C.   6, 18 _____       7, 21 _____        5, 25 _____

D.   4, 20 _____       8, 40 _____        3, 27 _____

E.   12, 18 _____      9, 36 _____

F.   5, 15 _____       24, 36 _____

G.   4, 24 _____       32, 40 _____

H.   3, 18 _____       20, 50 _____

I.   4, 16, 48 _____   6, 12, 36 _____

J.   7, 14, 28 _____   8, 16, 24 _____

# Wordy Fractions

**Equivalent fractions** have the same value.

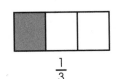 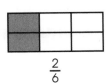 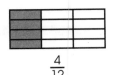

$$\frac{1}{3} \qquad \frac{2}{6} \qquad \frac{4}{12}$$

$$\frac{1}{3} = \frac{2}{6} = \frac{4}{12}$$

To find equivalent fractions, multiply the numerator and denominator by the same number.

$$\frac{1 \times 2}{3 \times 2} = \frac{2}{6} \qquad\qquad \frac{1 \times 4}{3 \times 4} = \frac{4}{12}$$

Write the letter of each equivalent fraction for the fractions below. Then, unscramble the letters to write a word. Use the Picture Clues for help.

| | | | | | | | |
|---|---|---|---|---|---|---|---|
| $\frac{6}{12}$ u | $\frac{2}{12}$ r | $\frac{10}{25}$ u | $\frac{4}{16}$ b | $\frac{4}{8}$ c | $\frac{12}{18}$ r | $\frac{16}{32}$ e | $\frac{4}{24}$ o |
| $\frac{14}{21}$ e | $\frac{7}{42}$ u | $\frac{12}{30}$ s | $\frac{4}{32}$ y | $\frac{3}{24}$ a | $\frac{8}{48}$ s | $\frac{6}{9}$ p | $\frac{3}{12}$ u |
| $\frac{6}{15}$ b | $\frac{3}{6}$ a | $\frac{10}{15}$ e | $\frac{2}{8}$ c | $\frac{8}{20}$ t | $\frac{5}{30}$ m | $\frac{8}{12}$ h | $\frac{14}{35}$ e |
| $\frac{5}{20}$ e | $\frac{2}{16}$ r | $\frac{3}{18}$ h | $\frac{4}{10}$ o | $\frac{6}{36}$ b | $\frac{2}{4}$ t | $\frac{4}{6}$ s | |

**Picture Clues**

$\frac{1}{2}$
$\frac{2}{3}$
$\frac{1}{4}$
$\frac{2}{5}$
$\frac{1}{8}$
$\frac{1}{6}$

$\frac{1}{2} = $ ___ ___ ___ ___
___

$\frac{2}{3} = $ ___ ___ ___ ___
___

$\frac{1}{4} = $ ___ ___ ___
___

$\frac{2}{5} = $ ___ ___ ___ ___
___

$\frac{1}{8} = $ ___ ___ ___

$\frac{1}{6} = $ ___ ___ ___ ___ ___
___

Math Practice: Grades 5–6

Name _____

# Everything Is Equal

To find an **equivalent fraction**, multiply or divide the numerator and denominator by the same number.

Find each equivalent fraction.

A. $\dfrac{2}{5} = \dfrac{}{10}$    $\dfrac{3}{4} = \dfrac{18}{}$    $\dfrac{3}{6} = \dfrac{}{24}$    $\dfrac{18}{36} = \dfrac{}{2}$    $\dfrac{20}{25} = \dfrac{}{5}$

B. $\dfrac{3}{4} = \dfrac{}{20}$    $\dfrac{1}{7} = \dfrac{}{49}$    $\dfrac{1}{4} = \dfrac{}{20}$    $\dfrac{12}{16} = \dfrac{3}{}$    $\dfrac{15}{35} = \dfrac{}{7}$

C. $\dfrac{1}{2} = \dfrac{}{8}$    $\dfrac{2}{5} = \dfrac{}{20}$    $\dfrac{2}{8} = \dfrac{}{16}$    $\dfrac{10}{100} = \dfrac{}{10}$    $\dfrac{15}{20} = \dfrac{3}{}$

D. $\dfrac{1}{3} = \dfrac{}{12}$    $\dfrac{1}{9} = \dfrac{}{81}$    $\dfrac{1}{5} = \dfrac{}{15}$

E. $\dfrac{1}{8} = \dfrac{}{16}$    $\dfrac{2}{11} = \dfrac{6}{}$    $\dfrac{2}{9} = \dfrac{}{27}$

F. $\dfrac{1}{6} = \dfrac{}{18}$    $\dfrac{1}{4} = \dfrac{8}{}$    $\dfrac{3}{5} = \dfrac{21}{}$

G.     $\dfrac{}{} = \dfrac{}{16}$

H. 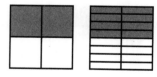    $\dfrac{}{} = \dfrac{}{16}$

I.     $\dfrac{}{} = \dfrac{}{15}$

Name _____

# Shading the Facts

To compare the fractions $\frac{1}{2}$ and $\frac{1}{3}$, follow these steps.

Find the least common multiples of 2 and 3.

multiples of 2 = 0, 2, 4, 6, 8, 10 . . .

multiples of 3 = 0, 3, 6, 9, 12 . . .

The LCM is 6. This becomes the least common denominator (LCD) of the two fractions.

Find equivalent fractions using the LCD. $\quad \frac{1}{2} = \frac{3}{6} \quad \frac{1}{3} = \frac{2}{6}$

Compare. $\quad \frac{3}{6} > \frac{2}{6}$ so $\frac{1}{2} > \frac{1}{3}$

When comparing fractions with the same numerator, the smaller the denominator, the greater the fraction.
  $\frac{1}{2} > \frac{1}{3}$

Identify each fraction. Compare using >, <, and =.

A. 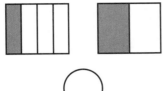 _____ ◯ _____   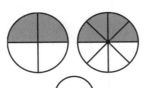 _____ ◯ _____   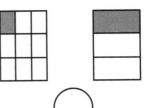 _____ ◯ _____

B. 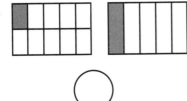 _____ ◯ _____   _____ ◯ _____   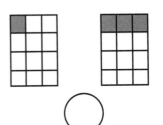 _____ ◯ _____

C. $\frac{1}{4}$ ◯ $\frac{1}{2}$    $\frac{6}{8}$ ◯ $\frac{1}{2}$    $\frac{4}{5}$ ◯ $\frac{6}{10}$    $\frac{1}{8}$ ◯ $\frac{1}{3}$

D. $\frac{1}{3}$ ◯ $\frac{1}{5}$    $\frac{2}{8}$ ◯ $\frac{1}{5}$    $\frac{1}{9}$ ◯ $\frac{1}{4}$    $\frac{1}{11}$ ◯ $\frac{1}{5}$

E. $\frac{1}{4}$ ◯ $\frac{1}{3}$    $\frac{1}{5}$ ◯ $\frac{1}{6}$    $\frac{2}{4}$ ◯ $\frac{1}{2}$    $\frac{3}{8}$ ◯ $\frac{1}{8}$

Name _____

# Finding the Fraction

What is $\frac{3}{4}$ of 12?

To find the fraction of a whole number, follow these steps.

Divide the whole number by the denominator. $12 \div 4 = 3$

Then, multiply by the numerator. $3 \times 3 = 9$

$\frac{3}{4}$ of 12 is 9.

Solve.

A. $\frac{2}{3}$ of 36        $\frac{1}{8}$ of 64        $\frac{3}{9}$ of 45        $\frac{2}{7}$ of 21        $\frac{5}{10}$ of 110

B. $\frac{7}{12}$ of 24        $\frac{9}{15}$ of 30        $\frac{1}{2}$ of 45        $\frac{4}{5}$ of 30        $\frac{2}{9}$ of 27

C. $\frac{4}{8}$ of 32        $\frac{1}{11}$ of 121        $\frac{3}{6}$ of 18        $\frac{1}{3}$ of 48        $\frac{3}{7}$ of 56

D. $\frac{4}{9}$ of 81        $\frac{3}{6}$ of 72        $\frac{4}{7}$ of 49

E. $\frac{1}{8}$ of 65        $\frac{3}{4}$ of 25        $\frac{1}{3}$ of 288

There are 64 squares on a board. 3/4 of them are shaded. How many squares are shaded?

Name _____

# Add It Up!

To add fractions with uncommon denominators, follow these steps.

$$\frac{1}{3} \quad \overline{12}$$
$$+\frac{2}{4} \quad \overline{12}$$

$$\frac{1 \times 4}{3 \times 4} = \frac{4}{12}$$
$$+\frac{2 \times 3}{4 \times 3} = \frac{6}{12}$$

$$\frac{4}{12}$$
$$+\frac{6}{12}$$
$$\frac{10}{12}$$

$$\frac{10 \div 2}{12 \div 2} = \frac{5}{6}$$

Find the least common denominator.

Make equivalent fractions.

Add.

Reduce to lowest terms.

## Add. Reduce to lowest terms.

A.
$$\frac{1}{3}$$
$$+\frac{2}{12}$$

$$\frac{3}{8}$$
$$+\frac{2}{16}$$

$$\frac{1}{5}$$
$$+\frac{3}{10}$$

$$\frac{1}{8}$$
$$+\frac{3}{16}$$

B.
$$\frac{4}{10}$$
$$+\frac{2}{20}$$

$$\frac{1}{6}$$
$$+\frac{3}{12}$$

$$\frac{1}{4}$$
$$+\frac{6}{8}$$

$$\frac{2}{5}$$
$$+\frac{4}{15}$$

C.
$$\frac{2}{7}$$
$$+\frac{1}{3}$$

$$\frac{1}{2}$$
$$+\frac{1}{8}$$

$$\frac{1}{5}$$
$$+\frac{1}{6}$$

$$\frac{1}{3}$$
$$+\frac{1}{4}$$

D.
$$\frac{1}{6}$$
$$+\frac{1}{9}$$

$$\frac{2}{8}$$
$$+\frac{1}{3}$$

$$\frac{3}{9}$$
$$+\frac{1}{2}$$

$$\frac{1}{4}$$
$$+\frac{3}{16}$$

Name _____

# Fraction Subtraction

To subtract fractions with unlike denominators, follow these steps.

$$\frac{2}{3} = \frac{}{6}$$
$$-\frac{2}{6} = -\frac{}{6}$$

$$\frac{2 \times 2}{3 \times 2} = \frac{4}{6}$$
$$\frac{2 \times 1}{6 \times 1} = \frac{2}{6}$$

$$\frac{4}{6}$$
$$-\frac{2}{6}$$
$$\frac{2}{6}$$

$$\frac{2 \div 2}{6 \div 2} = \frac{1}{3}$$

Find the least common denominator.

Make equivalent fractions.

Subtract.

Reduce to lowest terms.

Subtract. Reduce to lowest terms.

A.
$$\frac{7}{8} - \frac{2}{8}$$
$$\frac{1}{4} - \frac{1}{8}$$
$$\frac{1}{2} - \frac{3}{12}$$
$$\frac{4}{9} - \frac{1}{18}$$

B.
$$\frac{7}{10} - \frac{1}{5}$$
$$\frac{4}{12} - \frac{1}{6}$$
$$\frac{3}{4} - \frac{3}{8}$$
$$\frac{1}{2} - \frac{7}{14}$$

C.
$$\frac{3}{5} - \frac{1}{5}$$
$$\frac{1}{2} - \frac{1}{3}$$
$$\frac{1}{4} - \frac{1}{5}$$
$$\frac{1}{3} - \frac{1}{7}$$

D.
$$\frac{2}{3} - \frac{1}{5}$$
$$\frac{3}{4} - \frac{2}{5}$$
$$\frac{3}{7} - \frac{1}{8}$$
$$\frac{1}{2} - \frac{1}{9}$$

Name _____

# Fraction Frenzy

To multiply fractions, follow these steps.

$$\frac{1}{3} \times \frac{3}{5} = \frac{3}{15}$$

Multiply the numerators. Then, multiply the denominators.

$$\frac{3 \div 3}{15 \div 3} = \frac{1}{5}$$

Reduce to lowest terms.

Identify each fraction. Multiply. Reduce to lowest terms.

A. $\frac{2}{3}$ ×

$\frac{2}{3}$ × _____ = _____

B. $\frac{1}{2}$ ×

$\frac{1}{2}$ × _____ = _____

C. $\frac{1}{8}$ ×

$\frac{1}{8}$ × _____ = _____

D. $\frac{2}{3}$ ×

$\frac{2}{3}$ × _____ = _____

Multiply. Reduce to lowest terms.

E. $\frac{1}{3} \times \frac{1}{4}$     $\frac{1}{5} \times \frac{2}{6}$     $\frac{1}{9} \times \frac{1}{2}$     $\frac{1}{5} \times \frac{2}{3}$     $\frac{1}{2} \times \frac{3}{9}$

F. $\frac{1}{5} \times \frac{1}{6}$     $\frac{4}{5} \times \frac{1}{2}$     $\frac{1}{4} \times \frac{1}{3}$     $\frac{2}{5} \times \frac{1}{7}$     $\frac{3}{4} \times \frac{1}{5}$

G. $\frac{1}{6} \times \frac{1}{4}$     $\frac{3}{4} \times \frac{1}{7}$     $\frac{3}{5} \times \frac{1}{7}$     $\frac{1}{2} \times \frac{1}{3}$     $\frac{1}{2} \times \frac{2}{9}$

H. $\frac{3}{4} \times \frac{2}{7}$     $\frac{4}{8} \times \frac{1}{3}$     $\frac{1}{4} \times \frac{2}{6}$     $\frac{2}{3} \times \frac{1}{4}$     $\frac{1}{3} \times \frac{3}{9}$

Name _____

# Mixed Number Mix-Up

When adding or subtracting mixed numbers, follow these steps.

$3\frac{2}{5}$   $3\frac{4}{10}$   $3\frac{4}{10}$   $3\frac{4}{10}$

$+\ 4\frac{1}{10}$   $+\ 4\frac{1}{10}$   $+\ 4\frac{1}{10}$   $+\ 4\frac{1}{10}$   $7\frac{5}{10} = 7\frac{1}{2}$

   $\frac{5}{10}$   $7\frac{5}{10}$

Find a common denominator. Make equivalent fractions. | Add the fractions. | Add the whole numbers. | Reduce to lowest terms.

$6\frac{1}{2}$   $6\frac{6}{12}$   $6\frac{6}{12}$   $6\frac{6}{12}$

$-\ 2\frac{3}{12}$   $-\ 2\frac{3}{12}$   $-\ 2\frac{3}{12}$   $-\ 2\frac{3}{12}$   $4\frac{3}{12} = 4\frac{1}{4}$

   $\frac{3}{12}$   $4\frac{3}{12}$

Find a common denominator. Make equivalent fractions. | Subtract the fractions. | Subtract the whole numbers. | Reduce to lowest terms.

Add or subtract. Reduce to lowest terms.

A.   $2\frac{1}{5}$        $6\frac{1}{2}$        $5\frac{1}{2}$        $7\frac{1}{3}$        $18\frac{1}{4}$

$+\ 9\frac{1}{10}$   $+\ 2\frac{1}{4}$   $+\ 8\frac{1}{8}$   $+\ 3\frac{1}{4}$   $+\ 2\frac{3}{12}$

B.   $6\frac{1}{4}$        $10\frac{2}{3}$        $14\frac{2}{5}$        $8\frac{3}{4}$        $14\frac{7}{10}$

$+\ 8\frac{1}{2}$   $+\ 1\frac{1}{6}$   $+\ \ \frac{2}{5}$   $-\ 6\frac{1}{4}$   $-\ 7\frac{3}{10}$

C.   $9\frac{3}{5}$        $6\frac{4}{6}$        $8\frac{4}{8}$        $8\frac{3}{4}$        $5\frac{3}{4}$

$-\ 2\frac{1}{15}$   $-\ 3\frac{1}{3}$   $-\ 2\frac{1}{16}$   $-\ 2\frac{1}{2}$   $-\ 2\frac{1}{8}$

Name _____

# Fraction Flipping

To divide a whole number by a fraction, follow these steps.

$3 \div \frac{2}{4}$   $\frac{3}{1} \div \frac{2}{4}$          $\frac{2}{4} \circlearrowright \frac{4}{2}$          $\frac{3}{1} \times \frac{4}{2}$

Change the whole number to a fraction.

Find the reciprocal of the divisor by flipping the digits in the fraction.

Change the operation to multiplication and use the reciprocal instead of the divisor.

$\frac{3}{1} \times \frac{4}{2} = \frac{12}{2}$          $\frac{12}{2} = 6$          $3 \div \frac{2}{4} = 6$

Multiply.

Reduce to lowest terms.

**Divide. Reduce to lowest terms.**

A. $15 \div \frac{1}{3}$          $6 \div \frac{1}{12}$          $5 \div \frac{1}{10}$          $12 \div \frac{1}{10}$

B. $3 \div \frac{1}{8}$          $\frac{3}{5} \div \frac{1}{3}$          $\frac{1}{7} \div \frac{3}{4}$          $\frac{2}{6} \div \frac{1}{2}$

C. $\frac{2}{9} \div \frac{1}{3}$          $\frac{3}{12} \div \frac{1}{6}$

HEY! WHO ATE $3 \div 2/4$ OF MY MUFFINS?

D. $\frac{5}{10} \div \frac{1}{3}$          $\frac{2}{5} \div \frac{1}{9}$

E. $\frac{1}{8} \div \frac{1}{3}$          $\frac{8}{9} \div \frac{1}{3}$

**25**          Math Practice: Grades 5–6

Name _____

# Mix It Up!

To multiply mixed numbers, follow these steps.

$1\frac{2}{3} \times 1\frac{1}{2}$   $\frac{5}{3} \times \frac{3}{2}$        $\frac{5}{3} \times \frac{3}{2} = \frac{15}{6}$        $\frac{15}{6} = 2\frac{3}{6} = 2\frac{1}{2}$

Change each mixed number          Multiply.              Reduce to
to an improper fraction.                                 lowest terms.

To divide mixed numbers, follow these steps.

$3\frac{1}{2} \div 2$   $\frac{7}{2} \div 2$        $\frac{7}{2} \div \frac{2}{1}$        $\frac{7}{2} \times \frac{1}{2} = \frac{7}{4} = 1\frac{3}{4}$

Change the mixed      Change the       Turn the division problem into a multiplication
number to an          whole number     problem by finding the reciprocal of the divisor.
improper fraction.    to a fraction.   Multiply. Reduce to lowest terms if necessary.

Multiply or divide. Reduce to lowest terms.

A. $3\frac{1}{2} \times 3$        $4 \times 1\frac{1}{2}$        $5 \times 3\frac{1}{3}$        $2 \times 4\frac{1}{3}$

B. $1\frac{1}{3} \times 3\frac{1}{2}$        $1\frac{4}{5} \times 1\frac{2}{3}$        $1\frac{1}{4} \times 2\frac{1}{2}$        $\frac{1}{3} \times 1\frac{4}{8}$

C. $1\frac{3}{5} \div 4$        $2\frac{1}{2} \div 5$        $1\frac{2}{3} \div 2$        $3\frac{1}{4} \div 4$

D. $3\frac{1}{4} \div \frac{1}{2}$        $1\frac{1}{5} \div \frac{1}{4}$        $3\frac{4}{5} \div \frac{1}{2}$        $1\frac{2}{3} \div \frac{1}{3}$

E. $1\frac{1}{4} \times 1\frac{2}{4}$        $2\frac{1}{5} \times 1\frac{1}{2}$        $2\frac{1}{2} \div 1\frac{1}{3}$        $2\frac{1}{3} \div \frac{1}{6}$

Name _____

# Awesome Addends

| Add the ones column. Regroup. | Add each additional column, regrouping as you go. | Add a comma to the sum if appropriate. |
|---|---|---|
| 1<br>3,419<br>+ 2,138<br>———<br>7 | 1<br>3,419<br>+ 2,138<br>———<br>5557 | 1<br>3,419<br>+ 2,138<br>———<br>5,557 |

Add.

A.
| 349 | 671 | 746 | 1,214 | 3,125 |
|---|---|---|---|---|
| + 137 | + 849 | + 988 | + 837 | + 1,629 |

B.
| 7,642 | 9,106 | 5,219 | 7,100 | 7,649 |
|---|---|---|---|---|
| + 849 | + 928 | + 2,381 | + 3,699 | + 1,210 |

C.
| 5,432 | 2,314 | 5,614 | 314,120 | 389,146 |
|---|---|---|---|---|
| + 1,913 | + 1,789 | + 2,394 | + 8,349 | + 38 |

D.
| 341 | 2,142 | 6,438 | 5,102 | 4,216 |
|---|---|---|---|---|
| 122 | 1,325 | 1,002 | 4,342 | 1,312 |
| + 614 | + 1,519 | + 3,643 | + 1,628 | + 7,148 |

Name _____

# May I Borrow a Ten?

| Subtract the ones column. If necessary, borrow one ten. Regroup and subtract. | | Repeat until each column has been completed. | |
|---|---|---|---|
| $\overset{8}{5,2\cancel{9}\cancel{3}}$ <br> $-\ 2,764$ <br> 9 | $\overset{8\ 13}{5,2\cancel{9}\cancel{3}}$ <br> $-\ 2,764$ <br> 29 | $\overset{4\ 12\ 8\ 13}{\cancel{5}\cancel{2}\cancel{9}\cancel{3}}$ <br> $-\ 2,764$ <br> 529 | $\overset{4\ 12\ 8\ 13}{\cancel{5}\cancel{2}\cancel{9}\cancel{3}}$ <br> $-\ 2,764$ <br> 2,529 |

Subtract. Remember to borrow and regroup when needed.

A.
```
   300        594        347
 - 142      - 287      -  89
```

DO YOU THINK I COULD BORROW A TEN?

B.
```
   500      3,000      7,214
 - 247      -   29    - 1,807
```

C.
```
  6,432     4,312     5,148     7,642     7,647
- 2,518   - 1,927   -   329   -   808   -   927
```

D.
```
  5,412     6,294     3,412     6,200     7,645
- 1,384   - 3,912   -   987   -    98   - 1,328
```

E.
```
  36,004    49,248    316,149    317,142    418,147
- 12,762  - 21,853  -  21,302  - 192,316  - 121,389
```

Name _____

# What Is the Product?

|  |  |  |  |  |  |
|---|---|---|---|---|---|
| 2 1 | | 3 2 | | 1 1 | |
| 896 | 896 | 896 | 896 | 896 | 896 |
| x  243 | x  243 | x  243 | x  243 | x  243 | x  243 |
| 2688 | 2688 | 2688 | 2688 | 2688 | 2688 |
| | 0 | 35840 | 35840 | 35840 | 35840 |
| | | | 00 | 179200 | 179200 |
| | | | | | 217,728 |
| Multiply the ones digit (3) times 896. | Add a 0. | Multiply the tens digit (4) times 896. | Add two 0s. | Multiply the hundreds digit (2) times 896. | Add. Add the comma if needed. |

Multiply.

A.
```
      314          231          423          225          310
  x   231      x   312      x   125      x   234      x   204
```

B.
```
      132          124          101          318          283
  x   248      x   352      x   896      x   262      x   423
```

C.
```
    2,812        3,213        3,298        1,346        2,318
  x   342      x   546      x   112      x   241      x   192
```

# Get the Point

Name _____

When multiplying decimals, the sum total of digits to the right of the decimal point in each factor is the number of digits that will be to the right of the decimal point in the product.

|  | 2.014 | 2.014 |
|---|---|---|
|  | x  0.416 | x  0.416 |
|  | 12084 | 12084 |
|  | 20140 | 20140 |
|  | 805600 | 805600 |
|  | 0000000 | 0000000 |
|  | 0837824 | 0.837824 |

$$
\begin{array}{r} 2.014 \\ \underline{x\ \ 0.416} \end{array}
\quad
\begin{array}{l} \text{3 digits} \\ \underline{\text{3 digits}} \\ \text{6 digits} \end{array}
$$

Multiply.

A.

|  | 3.046 | 1.9 | 3.12 | 12.12 | 0.124 | 2.05 |
|---|---|---|---|---|---|---|
| x | 8 | 0.7 | 0.9 | 0.5 | 2 | 0.12 |

B.

|  | 12.12 | 2.115 | 54.21 | 8.8 | 2.416 | 213.1 |
|---|---|---|---|---|---|---|
| x | 3.4 | 24 | 1.31 | 1.92 | 28 | 3.9 |

Circle the products of the problems above. The numbers will go across and down.

| 2 | 4 | . | 3 | 6 | 8 | 9 | 4 | 7 | 1 | . | 0 | 1 | 5 | 1 | 9 | 6 | 8 | 1 | 3 |
|---|---|---|---|---|---|---|---|---|---|---|---|---|---|---|---|---|---|---|---|
| . | 0 | 5 | 5 | 8 | 3 | 1 | 2 | . | 3 | 4 | . | 6 | 7 | . | 6 | 4 | 8 | . | 6 |
| 6 | 7 | 1 | . | 6 | 1 | 9 | 8 | 2 | 3 | 7 | 2 | . | 8 | 5 | 1 | 1 | . | 3 | 3 |
| . | 6 | 4 | 5 | 1 | . | 8 | . | 0 | . | 2 | 4 | 8 | 2 | 3 | 7 | . | 9 | 4 | 5 |
| 3 | 4 | . | 9 | 2 | 0 | 8 | 9 | 2 | 6 | 5 | 6 | 9 | 4 | 2 | 4 | 2 | . | 2 | . |
| 3 | 2 | 1 | 1 | . | 9 | 0 | 2 | 5 | 0 | . | 7 | 6 | 3 | 6 | . | 0 | 6 | 7 | 8 |
| 1 | 4 | 9 | . | 1 | 2 | 1 | 7 | 8 | 9 | 1 | . | 5 | 2 | 2 | . | 8 | 0 | 8 | 9 |

Name _____

# Divide It Up

Divide 7 into 25. Multiply. Subtract. Bring down the next digit.

```
      3
7 ) 2586
  - 21 ↓
      48
```

Divide 7 into 48. Multiply. Subtract. Bring down the next digit.

```
     36
7 ) 2586
  - 21
     48
   - 42
     66
```

Divide 7 into 66. Multiply. Subtract. There are no more digits to bring down. The division is complete.

```
    369
7 ) 2586
  - 21
    48
  - 42
    66
  - 63
    3
```

The 3 becomes the remainder.

```
    369 R3
7 ) 2586
  - 21
    48
  - 42
    66
  - 63
    3
```

Divide.

A.  6 ) 50        4 ) 39        5 ) 44        9 ) 85        8 ) 43

B.  5 ) 227       7 ) 247       9 ) 420       4 ) 151       6 ) 539

C.  7 ) 2,887     4 ) 3,516     3 ) 2,396     7 ) 1,730     5 ) 2,329

Name _____

# Dynamite Division

Divide 25 into 41. Multiply. Subtract. Bring down the next digit.

```
      1
25 )41698
  - 25
    166
```

Divide 25 into 166. Multiply. Subtract. Bring down the next digit.

```
     16
25 )41698
  - 25
    166
  - 150
    169
```

Divide 25 into 169. Multiply. Subtract. Bring down the next digit.

```
     166
25 )41698
  - 25
    166
  - 150
    169
  - 150
    198
```

Divide 25 into 198. Multiply. Subtract. There are no more digits to bring down. The 23 becomes the remainder.

```
    1667 R 23
25 )41698
  - 25
    166
  - 150
    169
  - 150
    198
  - 175
    23
```

Divide.

A.  24 )220        31 )260        62 )330        58 )348        42 )340

B.  70 )630        38 )684        28 )753        57 )1,241      23 )1,449

C.  48 )15,085     44 )5,016      91 )11,557     52 )17,995     82 )10,302

Name _____

# Getting into Numbers

Divide 147 into 326.
Multiply. Subtract.
Bring down the
next digit.

```
        2
147 ) 32659
    - 294↓
      325
```

Divide 147 into 325.
Multiply. Subtract.
Bring down the
next digit.

```
       22
147 ) 32659
    - 294
      325
    - 294
      319
```

Divide 147 into 319.
Multiply. Subtract.

```
      222
147 ) 32659
    - 294
      325
    - 294
      319
    - 294
       25
```

There are no more
digits to bring down.
The 25 becomes the
remainder.

```
      222 R25
147 ) 32659
    - 294
      325
    - 294
      319
    - 294
       25
```

Divide.

A.  124 ) 1,116        225 ) 1,575        175 ) 3,750        124 ) 4,509

B.  103 ) 2,409        141 ) 15,933       42 ) 1,936         123 ) 38,757

C.  151 ) 19,327       210 ) 21,840       175 ) 39,600       210 ) 31,437

Name _____

# Zero Is a Hero

| Divide 36 into 38. Multiply. Subtract. Bring down the next digit. | 23 is not large enough to divide into. Place a 0 in the quotient. | Bring down the next digit. Divide 36 into 239. Multiply. Subtract. | There are no more digits to bring down. The 23 becomes the remainder. |
|---|---|---|---|
| $$\begin{array}{r} 1 \\ 36\overline{)3839} \\ -36\downarrow \\ \hline 23 \end{array}$$ | $$\begin{array}{r} 10 \\ 36\overline{)3839} \\ -36 \\ \hline 23 \end{array}$$ | $$\begin{array}{r} 106 \\ 36\overline{)3839} \\ -36 \\ \hline 239 \\ -216 \\ \hline 23 \end{array}$$ | $$\begin{array}{r} 106\ R23 \\ 36\overline{)3839} \\ -36 \\ \hline 239 \\ -216 \\ \hline 23 \end{array}$$ |

Divide. Watch for the zeros.

A. $8\overline{)167}$  $6\overline{)304}$  $4\overline{)363}$  $3\overline{)241}$  $9\overline{)638}$

B. $7\overline{)846}$  $4\overline{)827}$  $6\overline{)785}$  $8\overline{)1,657}$  $5\overline{)2,104}$

C. $35\overline{)3,604}$  $28\overline{)3,360}$  $19\overline{)8,568}$  $64\overline{)8,383}$  $32\overline{)8,964}$

# Decimal Division

Multiply both the divisor and the dividend by a number that frees the divisor of decimals. (Use 100 to move the decimal point over two places to the right.)

$1.32 \overline{)35.772}$    $132 \overline{)3577.2}$

Line up the decimal point and place it in the quotient.

$132 \overline{)3577.2}$

Begin dividing.

```
        27.1
132 )3577.2
    -246
     937
    -924
     132
    -132
       0
```

Divide.

A.  $3 \overline{)5.4}$    $4 \overline{)10.4}$    $7 \overline{)25.9}$    $6 \overline{)27.6}$    $0.2 \overline{)17.8}$

B.  $3.4 \overline{)80.24}$    $2.5 \overline{)114.75}$    $1.9 \overline{)149.15}$    $3.8 \overline{)262.58}$    $5.1 \overline{)196.86}$

C.  $0.18 \overline{)1.134}$    $0.46 \overline{)1.2788}$    $0.14 \overline{)5.152}$

Name _____

# Two-Step Stumpers

The following word problem requires two different steps to solve.

David wants to buy enough flour so that everyone in the class can make a salt dough model of a landform. A 5 lb. bag of flour costs $.42 per lb. and will serve 7 students. How many pounds will he need for 28 students? What will be the total cost?

Step one:
Set up a proportion. $\frac{5}{7} = \frac{n}{28}$   n = 20

Total pounds needed: 20 lb.

Step two:
Figure the total cost.

$$\begin{array}{r} \$.42 \\ \times\ 20 \\ \hline \$8.40 \end{array}$$

Total cost: $8.40

Solve each two-step problem.

A. The temperature outside right now is 0° C. It is 7:00 A.M. If the temperature rises 2 degrees every hour, what will the temperature be at 12:00 noon? _____ If it then drops 1 degree every hour after that, what time will it be when it returns to 0° C? _____

B. Miguel has permission to buy 10 apples at $.40 each. If he gives the cashier $10.00, how much change will he get? _____

C. Eva has collected 3 bags of seashells, with 18 shells in each bag. How many more shells does she need to collect to have a total of 75 shells? _____

D. Chin Lee is 11 years old. Her parents have saved $40.00 for each of her 11 birthdays. How many more birthdays are needed before Chin Lee has over $500.00 saved? _____ How much will she have saved? _____

E. Mark loves to hike with his dad. They hike the challenging Grand Canyon every year in January for 3 days. If they hike for 96 hours on this trip, how many more days have they hiked than usual? _____

F. It takes Monica 2 hours to complete one drawing. She earns $5.00 per drawing. How many hours will she have to draw to earn $15.00? _____

Name _____

# Too Much Information

Sometimes there is too much information in a word problem. The irrelevant information is not needed to solve the problem.

Mia needs 4 cups of flour to make homemade bread. She also needs 3 cups of masa to make tortillas. If the recipe calls for 1 tablespoon of seasoning for each cup of flour, how many tablespoons will she need? To solve this problem, which statement is not relevant? The information about the masa needed to make tortillas is not relevant.

Cross out the unneeded information. Solve.

A. Josiah has a pet turtle that eats 5 carrots a week. He also has a pet frog. If carrots cost $.25 each, how much does it cost Josiah each week to feed his turtle?

B. Andy's dad is boiling 2 quarts of water on the stove. He is also cooking 5 rolls in the microwave. He is going to use 1 pint of the boiling water for his tea. How many pints of boiling water will be left over to use for his soup?

C. One-third of Alexa's pencils are blue. Silver is her favorite color of pencils. If Alexa has a total of 15 pencils, how many are blue?

D. Samuel has a total of 30 fish in his fish tank. Most are small, but some are large. If 10% are neon colors, how many is that in all?

E. It takes Heather 15 minutes to walk home from school. It takes her 10 minutes to walk from home to her friend Gwen's house. If school is out at 2:50 P.M., what time does she arrive home?

F. Steve's parents are very proud of how he uses his monthly allowance. Steve spends a total of $3.00 each month on fun stuff at the local dollar store. He saves $8.00 in the bank and donates $4.00 to the local food bank. His favorite sport is softball. He spends 3 hours a week practicing. How much money is Steve's allowance each month?

G. Tom and Jim love to catch tadpoles at the local pond. They raise them and then release them back into the pond. This year they have raised a total of 35 tadpoles. Their dads go fishing for two hours each time they are at the pond. If Tom and Jim continue to raise tadpoles each year, how many will they have raised in 3 years?

**45**

Math Practice: Grades 5–6

# What's the Operation?

Choose the operation. Solve the problem.

A. Juan has $3.67 to spend at the store. His friend Esteban has $6.25. How much do they have altogether?

B. Sing and the student council have collected 492 pounds of food for local families in need. If she divides the food equally between 6 families, how much food will each family receive?

C. Recently, ⅓ of the students at Washington Elementary School had perfect scores on a test. An additional ¼ of the students performed almost as well. What fraction of the students scored well on the test?

D. Zoe found out that there were 6 groups in her science class. Each group was composed of 7 students. How many students were there in all?

E. Gwen and Tom have a great idea! They plan to save a total of $50.00 to buy clothing for the local shelter in their city. Right now they have a total of $36.89. How much more do they need to save to reach their goal?

F. Leandra and Shayla are so excited about the drive to support hungry children that they promoted at their school. Generous fifth and sixth graders at their school donated a total of $214.55 to the drive. The girls just found out that the department store near the school will add 6 times the total of what they collected. How much will the department store be contributing?

# The Fact Family

| Addition and subtraction are related operations. | Multiplication and division are related operations. |
|---|---|
| $8 + 7 = 15$ | $0.5 \times 0.7 = 0.35$ |
| $7 + 8 = 15$ | $0.7 \times 0.5 = 0.35$ |
| $15 - 8 = 7$ | $0.35 \div 0.5 = 0.7$ |
| $15 - 7 = 8$ | $0.35 \div .7 = .5$ |

Each group of number sentences is called a **fact family**.

Write the fact family for each set of numbers. Use addition and subtraction.

A.  8, 12, 20

_____

_____

_____

_____

B.  25, 32, 57

_____

_____

_____

_____

C.  $\frac{3}{9}$,  $\frac{4}{9}$,  $\frac{7}{9}$

_____

_____

_____

_____

D. 0.4, 0.8, 1.2

_____

_____

_____

_____

E.  3.2, 4.8, 8

_____

_____

_____

_____

F.  $\frac{3}{11}$,  $\frac{6}{11}$,  $\frac{9}{11}$

_____

_____

_____

_____

Write the fact family for each set of numbers. Use multiplication and division.

G.  7, 8, 56

_____

_____

_____

_____

H.  0.5, 0.8, 0.40

_____

_____

_____

_____

I.  $\frac{1}{3}$,  $\frac{1}{2}$,  $\frac{1}{6}$

_____

_____

_____

_____

Math Practice: Grades 5–6

Name _____

# Estimation Station

**Estimate** to get an approximate answer. To estimate, round each number to its greatest place value.

| | | | | | | | | | |
|---|---|---|---|---|---|---|---|---|---|
| 89 | 90 | 742 | 700 | 8.96 | 9 | 524 | 500 | 11.8 | 12 |
| + 23 | + 20 | − 361 | − 400 | + 1.32 | + 1 | x  6 | x  6 | 5)59 | 5)60 |
| 112 | 110 | 381 | 300 | 10.28 | 10 | 3,144 | 3,000 | | |
| addition | | subtraction | | decimals | | multiplication | | division | |

Estimate the answer to each problem. Then, find the actual answer and compare.

A.
```
    389
+   232      + _____
```

B.
```
     76
+    29      + _____
```

C.
```
   6,841
+  2,399     + _____
```

D.
```
    698
−   465      − _____
```

E.
```
     48
−    39      − _____
```

F.
```
   3,486
−  1,978     − _____
```

G.
```
    6.48
+   3.92     + _____
```

H.
```
   34.92
x      5     x _____
```

I.
```
   32.99
+  16.24     + _____
```

J.
```
    824
x      5     x _____
```

K.
```
     69
x     24     x _____
```

L.
```
   8,142
x      9     x _____
```

M.
```
6)192
```

N.
```
5)1,390
```

O.
```
29)8,642
```

Name _____

# In the Ballpark

Front-end estimating is one way to get an approximate "ballpark" sum.

| $3.29 | 1. Add the dollars. | 2. Group the cents. | 3. Estimate. |
|---|---|---|---|
| $1.84 | 3 | $3.29 \\ $1.84 } about $1 | $10 + $2 = $12 |
| + $6.84 | 1 | + $6.84 — about $1 | |
| | + 6 | | |
| | $10 | | |

Estimate using front-end estimation. Find the actual answer and compare.

A.
```
  $3.29          624          3,214
+  1.89  ___   + 192  ___   + 1,849  ___
```

B.
```
  4,216        2,416          325
+ 1,842  ___  + 1,721  ___  +  102  ___
```

C.
```
  $7.28        $2.06         $7.86
   3.64         3.43          2.84
+  2.87  ___  + 1.57  ___   + 1.92  ___
```

D.
```
   314         $3.10         1,294
   168          1.72         3,762
   152          3.48         1,346
+  349  ___   + 2.69  ___  + 2,688  ___
```

Name _____

# Repeat After Me

Complete each pattern.

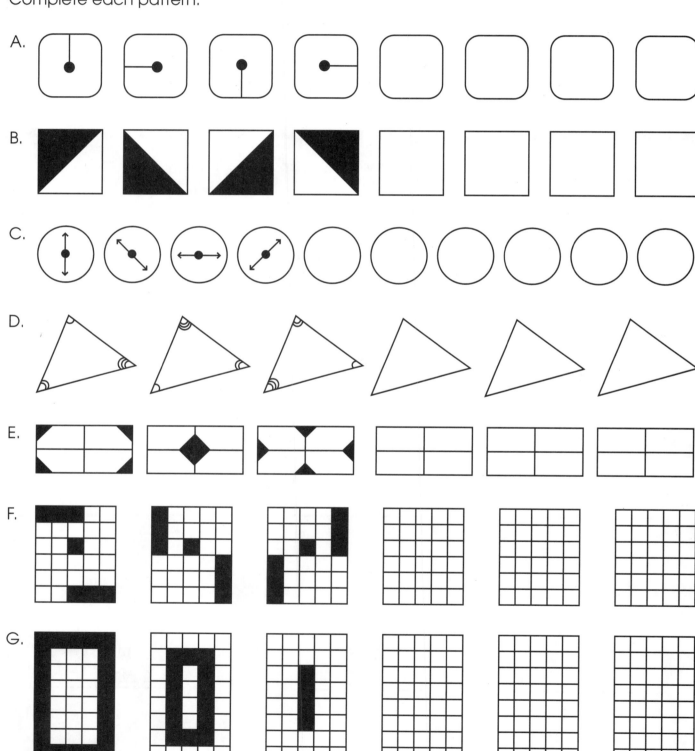

Name _____

# The Difference Is in the Count

What kind of pattern is shown in this set of numbers?

1 + 1 = 2
2 + 2 = 4
3 + 3 = 6
4 + 4 = 8
5 + 5 = 10
6 + 6 = 12
7 + 7 = 14

What would the next equation be in this pattern?  8 + 8 = 16

Each of the sums are a multiple of what number?  2

What is the difference between each sum?  2

HEY! IF YOU HAVE SIX MORE CARS, WE CAN GET A PATTERN GOING HERE!

Use patterns A.–F. to complete the table.

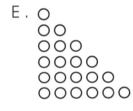

A. B. C. D. E. F.

Number of circles on the bottom row.

Number of circles on the bottom row and left column.

Total circles in each triangle.

Difference between the total number of circles in each triangle and the next triangle.

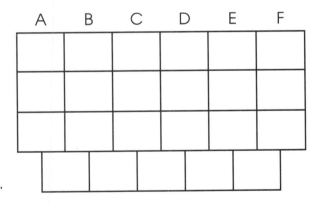

| | A | B | C | D | E | F |
|---|---|---|---|---|---|---|
| | | | | | | |
| | | | | | | |
| | | | | | | |

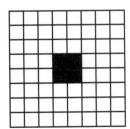 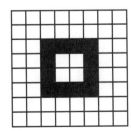 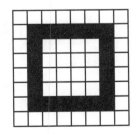 

What is the total number of shaded squares in each design. _____ _____ _____ _____

What is the difference between each set of shaded squares? _____

© Carson-Dellosa CD-4327          **51**          Math Practice: Grades 5–6

Name _____

# Sometimes It Is Up, Up, and Away

0, 7, 14, 21, 28, 35, ____, ____, ____
Look for the pattern in the numeric sequence.
0, 7, 14, 21, 28, 35, 42, 49, 56
Each number increases by 7.

Look at the pattern on the graph. If the pattern continues, what will be the next three entries on the graph? 9, 12, 15

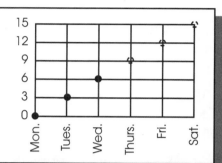

Write the next three numbers for each pattern.

A. 25, 20, 15, ____, ____, ____

B. 0.5, 1.0, 1.5, ____, ____, ____,

C. $\frac{1}{3}$, $\frac{2}{6}$, $\frac{3}{9}$, $\frac{4}{12}$, ____, ____, ____

D. 1, 4, 9, 16, ____, ____, ____

Write the rule for each table and then complete.

E. Rule:

| 3 | 6 |
|---|---|
| 4 | 8 |
| 5 | 10 |
| 6 | |
| 7 | |
| 8 | |
| 9 | |

F. Rule:

| 3 | 1 |
|---|---|
| 6 | 2 |
| 9 | 3 |
| 12 | |
| 15 | |
| 18 | |
| 21 | |

G. Rule:

| 1 | 0.25 |
|---|------|
| 2 | 0.5 |
| 3 | 0.75 |
| 4 | |
| 5 | |
| 6 | |
| 7 | |

H. Rule:

| 0 | 5 |
|---|---|
| 1 | 6 |
| 2 | 7 |
| 3 | 8 |
| 4 | |
| 5 | |
| 6 | |

I. Rule:

| 0.1 | 0.6 |
|-----|-----|
| 0.2 | 0.7 |
| 0.3 | 0.8 |
| 0.4 | |
| 0.5 | |
| 0.6 | |
| 0.7 | |

Find the pattern for each graph and then complete.

J.

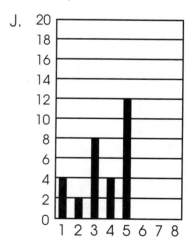

K.

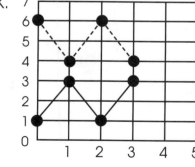

L.

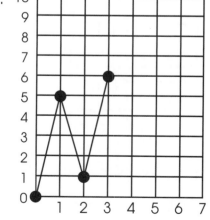

Name _____

# Wormy Addition

| Commutative Property of Addition: | Commutative Property of Multiplication: |
|---|---|
| $3 + 4 = 7$ <br> $4 + 3 = 7$ <br> $4 + 3 = 3 + 4$ | $5 \times 4 = 20$ <br> $4 \times 5 = 20$ <br> $4 \times 5 = 5 \times 4$ |
| **Associative Property of Addition:** | **Associative Property of Multiplication:** |
| $3 + (4 + 5) = 12$ <br> $(3 + 4) + 5 = 12$ | $2 \times (3 \times 4) = 24$ <br> $(2 \times 3) \times 4 = 24$ |

**Distributive Property of Multiplication Over Addition:**

$8 \times (3 + 2) = (8 \times 3) + (8 \times 2)$

Identify the property as either **commutative**, **associative**, or **distributive**.

A. $7 + 1.8 = 8.8$
$1.8 + 7 = 8.8$

_____

C. $(4 \times 8) \times 2 = 64$
$4 \times (8 \times 2) = 64$

_____

E. $\frac{2}{4} + \frac{1}{4} = \frac{3}{4}$

$\frac{1}{4} + \frac{2}{4} = \frac{3}{4}$

_____

B. $6 \times (8 + 1) = (6 \times 8) + (6 \times 1)$

_____

D. $(2 + 4) + 3 = 9$
$2 + (4 + 3) = 9$

_____

F. $2 \times (3 + 5) = (2 \times 3) + (2 \times 5)$

_____

G. $3.5 + 2.3 = 5.8$
$2.3 + 3.5 = 5.8$

_____

H. Write the equations that go with the word problem. Then, tell which property is being identified.

Al went to the store for his mom and purchased 5 apples and 7 oranges. Starting with the 5 apples, he added the fruit together. The total equaled 12. At home, his mom added the fruit together starting with the 7 oranges. Again, the total equaled 12.

Both equations: _____    _____

Property: _____

Name _____

# It Is All Commutative

3 + 4 = 7

4 + 3 = 7

5 x 4 = 20     4 x 5 = 20

**Commutative Property of Addition:**
3 + 4 = 4 + 3

**Commutative Property of Multiplication:**
5 x 4 = 4 x 5

Write each equation to show the commutative property of addition.

A. ⬜⬜⬜⬜⬜ + ⬜⬜

_____

⬜ + ⬜⬜⬜⬜⬜

_____

B. ⬜⬜⬜ + ⬜⬜⬜⬜⬜⬜⬜⬜

_____

⬜⬜⬜⬜⬜⬜⬜⬜ + ⬜⬜⬜

_____

C. ⬛⬛⬜⬜⬜⬜⬜⬜ + ⬛⬛⬜⬜

_____

⬛⬜⬜⬜ + ⬛⬛⬜⬜⬜⬜⬜⬜

_____

D. ▦ + ▦

_____

▦ + ▦

_____

Write each equation to show the commutative property of multiplication.

E.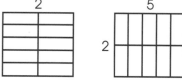

_____   _____

F.

_____   _____

Associative
property of
addition and
multiplication

# Associative Properties

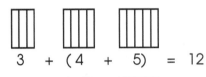

3 + ( 4 + 5) = 12

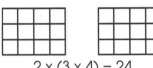

2 x (3 x 4) = 24

(3 + 4) + 5 = 12

(2 x 3) x 4 = 24

**Associative Property of Addition**    **Associative Property of Multiplication**

Write each equation to show the associative property of addition.

A. ▦ + ( ▦ + ▦ )

_____

( ▦ + ▦ ) + ▦

_____

B. ▦ + ( ▦ + ▭ )

_____

( ▦ + ▦ ) + ▭

_____

C. ▭ + ( ▭ + ▦ )

_____

( ▭ + ▭ ) + ▦

_____

D. ▯ + ( ▭ + ▦ )

_____

( ▯ + ▭ ) + ▦

_____

Write each equation to show the associative property of multiplication.

E. ▦ ▦ ▦

_____

▦ ▦ ▦ ▦ ▦

_____

Name _____

# Distribution Time

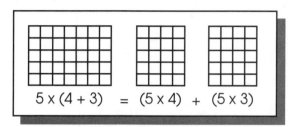

$$5 \times (4 + 3) = (5 \times 4) + (5 \times 3)$$

Write an equation showing the distributive property for each diagram.

A.
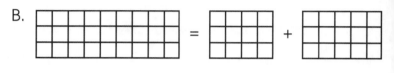

_____

B.

_____

C.

_____

D.
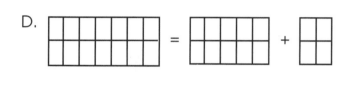

_____

Name _____

# Equation Maze

| | | |
|---|---|---|
| $m - 6 = 10$    (+ 6) | $m - 6 + 6 = 10 + 6$ | $m = 16$ |
| To solve for the variable, always use the inverse operation on both sides of the equation. | Add 6 to both sides (+ 6). | Add. |
| $n + 7 = 12$    (– 7) | $n + 7 - 7 = 12 - 7$ | $n = 5$ |
| Use the inverse operation on both sides of the equation. | Subtract 7 from both sides (– 7). | Subtract. |

Find the value of the variable. Travel the paths to link each correct answer with its equation.

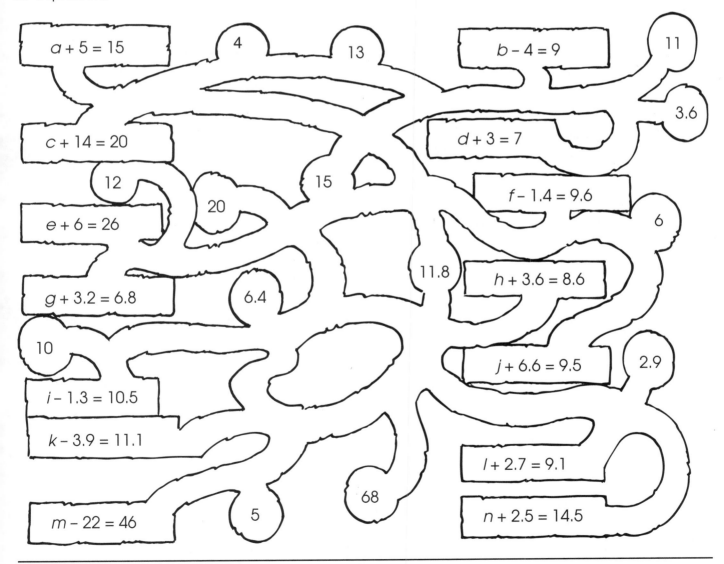

Name _____

# Mirror Images

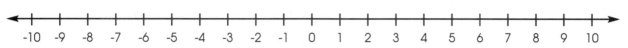

-10  -9  -8  -7  -6  -5  -4  -3  -2  -1  0  1  2  3  4  5  6  7  8  9  10

The numbers on each side of 0 are **integers**. Zero is also an integer.

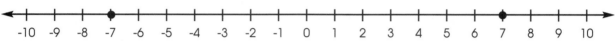

-10  -9  -8  -7  -6  -5  -4  -3  -2  -1  0  1  2  3  4  5  6  7  8  9  10

For every number on the number line, there is an opposite on the other side of 0.
So, the opposite of 7 is -7, and the opposite of 0 is 0.

Follow the directions to circle the number on each number line. Then, circle its opposite.
Write it on the blank.

A.  Circle 10.                                    Opposite: _____

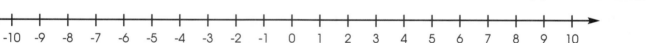

-10  -9  -8  -7  -6  -5  -4  -3  -2  -1  0  1  2  3  4  5  6  7  8  9  10

B.  Circle 5.                                     Opposite: _____

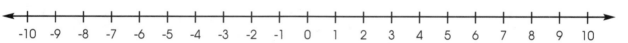

-10  -9  -8  -7  -6  -5  -4  -3  -2  -1  0  1  2  3  4  5  6  7  8  9  10

C.  Circle -6.                                    Opposite: _____

-10  -9  -8  -7  -6  -5  -4  -3  -2  -1  0  1  2  3  4  5  6  7  8  9  10

D.  Circle -9.                                    Opposite: _____

-10  -9  -8  -7  -6  -5  -4  -3  -2  -1  0  1  2  3  4  5  6  7  8  9  10

E.  Circle 8.                                     Opposite: _____

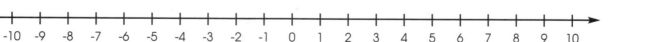

-10  -9  -8  -7  -6  -5  -4  -3  -2  -1  0  1  2  3  4  5  6  7  8  9  10

F.  Circle 3.                                     Opposite: _____

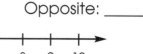

-10  -9  -8  -7  -6  -5  -4  -3  -2  -1  0  1  2  3  4  5  6  7  8  9  10

Name _____

# Positively Larger

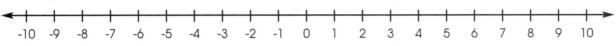
-10 -9 -8 -7 -6 -5 -4 -3 -2 -1 0 1 2 3 4 5 6 7 8 9 10

4 > -5   A positive number is always greater than a negative number.
The integer with the greatest value is the number farthest to the right on a number line.

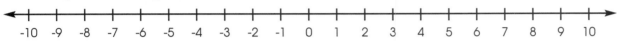
-10 -9 -8 -7 -6 -5 -4 -3 -2 -1 0 1 2 3 4 5 6 7 8 9 10

With two negative numbers, the greater number is the integer closer to 0.
-3 > -10   (Note that -3 is to the right of -10.)

Compare. Write >, <, or =.

A.  -5 ◯ -2      10 ◯ -2      -4 ◯ 3      8 ◯ 2      9 ◯ 3

B.  7 ◯ -12      10 ◯ 10      2 ◯ -12      3 ◯ -3      -5 ◯ 1

C.  -6 ◯ 2      -8 ◯ 10      4 ◯ -11      -9 ◯ -9      6 ◯ 8

D.  7 ◯ -6      5 ◯ -8      -3 ◯ -2      10 ◯ 4      -2 ◯ -1

Identify each temperature reading. Circle the warmer temperature.

E. 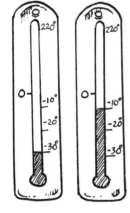     F. 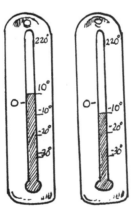     G. 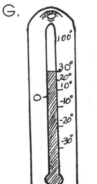     H.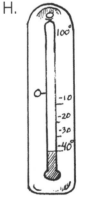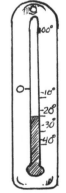

___°F ___°F       ___°F ___°F       ___°C ___°C       ___°C ___°C

     Math Practice: Grades 5–6

Name _____

# Movement by Steps

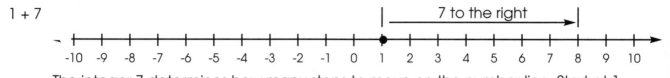

1 + 7          7 to the right

The integer 7 determines how many steps to move on the number line. Start at 1. Since the integer 7 is positive, move to the right 7 steps.

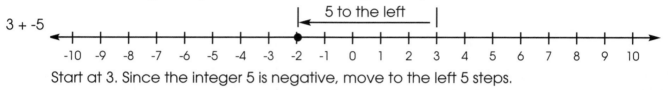

3 + -5          5 to the left

Start at 3. Since the integer 5 is negative, move to the left 5 steps.

Write the integer that identifies the movement on the number line.

A.

Movement: _____

B.
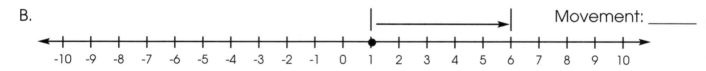
Movement: _____

C.

Movement: _____

Find the beginning point (marked by a square). Move the number of steps that the integer represents. Place a dot at the new point and write the new position.

D. +8

New Position: _____

E. -8
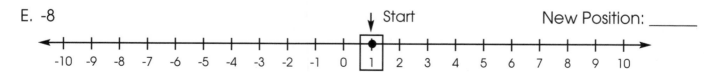
New Position: _____

F. +10

New Position: _____

Name _____

# Make the Right Move

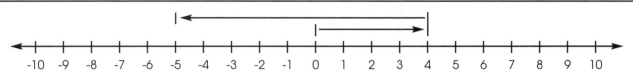

Example: 4 + -9 = -5

Begin at 0. Move to the right 4 steps. Then move to the left 9 steps. The final destination
is the sum -5.

**Positive integers** move to the right. ⟶

**Negative integers** move to the left. ⟵

Use the number line to find each sum. Example: -4 + -2 = -6

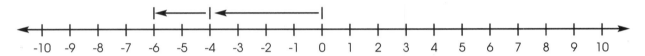

A. 8 + -7 = _____          -3 + 4 = _____          -9 + -2 = _____          7 + 2 = _____

B. -11 + 2 = _____          9 + -10 = _____          -4 + 7 = _____          -6 + 4 = _____

C. 8 + 6 = _____          -4 + 9 = _____          3 + -2 = _____          -9 + 2 = _____

D. 10 + -7 = _____          11 + -10 = _____          -8 + 4 = _____          -5 + 8 = _____

E. -8 + 3 = _____          -3 + 12 = _____          -10 + 8 = _____          -1 + 8 = _____

Circle the correct equation shown on each number line. Solve.

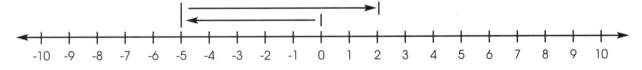

F. 2 + -5 = _____          -5 + 7 = _____          -5 + 2 = _____          7 + 2 = _____

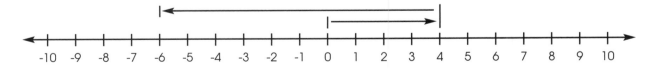

G. -6 + 4 = _____          -10 + 4 = _____          4 + -6 = _____          4 + -10 = _____

Name _____

# Switcheroo

To subtract integers, switch the sign and add the opposite. Example: 5 – -3 = _____
Step 1: Change the integer -3 to a +3 (the opposite).  5 – + = _____
Step 2: Now change the operation to addition:  5 + 3 = _____      5 + 3 = 8
(These steps must be done at the same time or the value of the expression will change.)

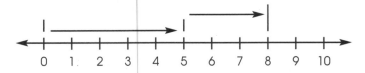

Use the number line to find each sum. Example: -3 – -9 = 6

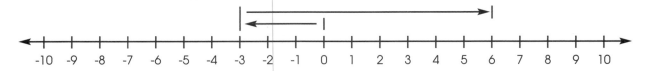

A. 8 – -4 = _____     -9 – -3 = _____     8 – 4 = _____     -7 – -5 = _____

B. 4 – -9 = _____     5 – -8 = _____     -4 – -8 = _____     2 – -2 = _____

C. -6 – -2 = _____     11 – -7 = _____     7 – 5 = _____     4 – -6 = _____

D. 9 – -5 = _____     -4 – -3 = _____     -5 – -1 = _____     3 – -8 = _____

E. -8 – 4 = _____     -2 – -12 = _____     -7 – -15 = _____     -7 – -11 = _____

F. -10 – 3 = _____     -11 – -5 = _____     -9 – 3 = _____     5 – -12 = _____

7 - -3 = 7 + 3 = 10

Math Practice: Grades 5–6

Name _____

# Order Us Around

Use the following order to solve and calculate expressions:
1. Simplify each exponent to standard form. $(6^2 \div 12) \times 2 + 3 \rightarrow (36 \div 12) \times 2 + 3$
2. Solve inside parentheses. $(36 \div 12) \times 2 + 3 \rightarrow (3) \times 2 + 3$
3. Multiply and divide from left to right. $3 \times 2 + 3 \rightarrow 6 + 3$
4. Add and subtract from left to right. $6 + 3 \rightarrow 9$

Solve each expression. Remember to follow the order of operations.

A.  $(6 \times 2) + 8 =$ _____   $3 + (8 \times 2) =$ _____

B.  $14 \div 2 + 3 =$ _____   $21 \div 7 \times 2 =$ _____

C.  $(5 \times 2) + 3 =$ _____   $(10 + 10) \div 2 =$ _____

D.  $6 \times (3 + 3) =$ _____   $10 \times 10 \div 25 =$ _____

E.  $(17 - 7) \div 5 =$ _____   $50 \div 5 + 3 =$ _____

F.  $8 - 2 + 9 =$ _____   $18 \div 9 + 3 =$ _____

G.  $(15 \div 3) \times 5 =$ _____   $(45 \div 9) \times 4 =$ _____

H.  $5 + (21 + 4) =$ _____   $15 - 2 + 8 =$ _____

I.  $40 \div 5 - 7 =$ _____   $(5 \times 7) - 30 =$ _____

J.  $(4 \times 4) + 5 =$ _____   $21 \div 7 + 3 =$ _____

K.  $(2^2 - 2) \times 3 + 8 =$ _____   $(15 \times 2) \div 10 + 8 =$ _____

L.  $10 - (14 \div 2) + 3 =$ _____   $2 \times 2 \div 2 \times 8 =$ _____

# Time to Review

A. Write the word name for 345,123.

_____

B. Figure 20% of 100.

C. Write the value of $2^4$.

D. Convert $\frac{2}{5}$ to a decimal.

E. Convert $\frac{30}{100}$ to a percent.

F. What is $\frac{2}{5}$ of 25?

G. What is $\frac{3}{5}$ of 25?

H. Add.
$$\frac{1}{4}$$
$$+ \frac{2}{8}$$

I. Subtract.
$$6$$
$$- 3\frac{1}{3}$$

J. Estimate using front-end estimation.
$$\begin{array}{r} \$2.45 \\ 3.59 \\ 1.32 \\ + \ 8.89 \end{array}$$

K. Add.
$$\begin{array}{r} 3,148 \\ 2,462 \\ + \ 5,130 \end{array}$$

L. Multiply.
$$\begin{array}{r} 3.194 \\ \times \quad 6 \end{array}$$

M. Divide.
$$8\overline{)28.8}$$

N. Multiply.
$$\begin{array}{r} 482 \\ \times \quad 23 \end{array}$$

O. Divide.
$$6\overline{)2,736}$$

# Time to Review

A. Write the word name for 345,123.

_____

B. Figure 20% of 100.

C. Write the value of $2^4$.

D. Convert $\frac{2}{5}$ to a decimal.

E. Convert $\frac{30}{100}$ to a percent.

F. What is $\frac{2}{5}$ of 25?

G. What is $\frac{3}{5}$ of 25?

H. Add.
$$\frac{1}{4} + \frac{2}{8}$$

I. Subtract.
$$6 - 3\frac{1}{3}$$

J. Estimate using front-end estimation.
$$\begin{array}{r}\$2.45\\3.59\\1.32\\+\ 8.89\end{array}$$

K. Add.
$$\begin{array}{r}3{,}148\\2{,}462\\+\ 5{,}130\end{array}$$

L. Multiply.
$$\begin{array}{r}3.194\\\times\quad6\end{array}$$

M. Divide.
$$8\overline{)28.8}$$

N. Multiply.
$$\begin{array}{r}482\\\times\quad23\end{array}$$

O. Divide.
$$6\overline{)2{,}736}$$

© Carson-Dellosa CD-4327  64  Math Practice: Grades 5–6

Name _____

P. Identify the multiplication equation.

_____ = _____

Q. Complete the pattern.

0, 4, 8, 12, _____, _____, _____

R. Solve for $n$.

$n + 2.9 = 10$

S. Complete the sentence. Use **>**, **<**, or **=**.

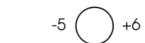

-5 ◯ +6

Use the number line to solve.

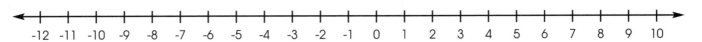

-12 -11 -10 -9 -8 -7 -6 -5 -4 -3 -2 -1 0 1 2 3 4 5 6 7 8 9 10

T. $-8 + -4 =$ _____

U. $5 - -8 =$ _____

Solve each expression.

V. $(3^2 + 3) \div 2 \times 3$

W. $(4^2 + 4) + 4 - 5$

X. How does a number line help you add or subtract integers?

_____

_____

_____

Y. Write an expression with a value of 20 using at least four numbers. Remember the order of operations.

Name _____

# What Am I?

Use the Word Bank to help complete the crossword puzzle.

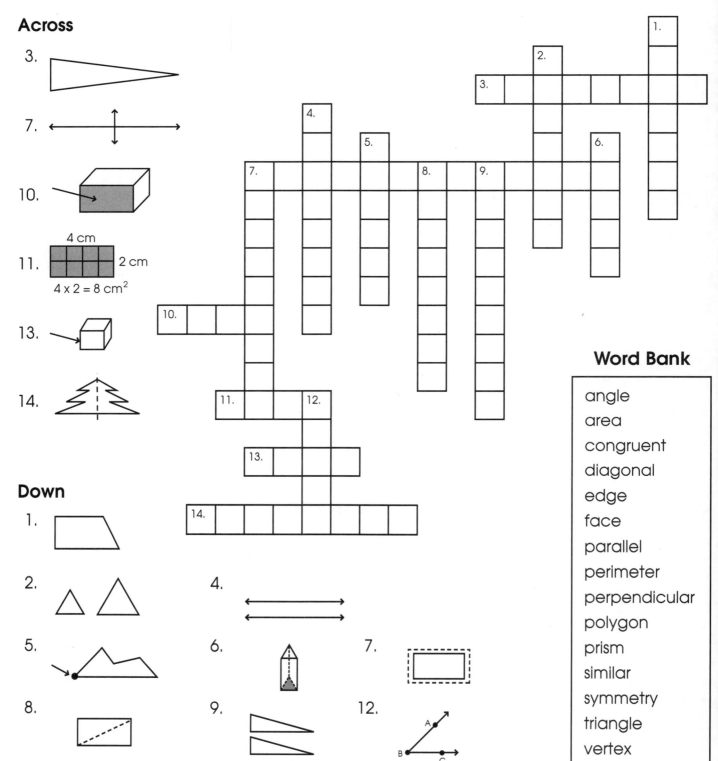

## Across

3.

7.

10.

11. 4 cm | 2 cm
$4 \times 2 = 8 \text{ cm}^2$

13.

14.

## Down

1.

2.

4.

5.

6.

7.

8.

9.

12.

## Word Bank

angle
area
congruent
diagonal
edge
face
parallel
perimeter
perpendicular
polygon
prism
similar
symmetry
triangle
vertex

Name _____

# Seeing Stars

There are 4 quadrants on a **coordinate grid**.

| Q2 | Q1 |
|----|----|
| Q3 | Q4 |

There is an *x*-axis and a *y*-axis. Follow the *x*-axis first, then the *y*-axis.

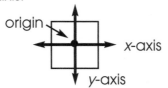

origin

*x*-axis

*y*-axis

Plot (-3, 2)

Start at the origin. Use the ordered pair to find the location on the grid. Follow the *x*-axis first, then the *y*-axis.

(left 3, up 2)

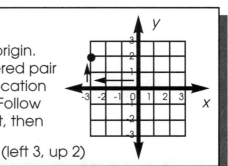

Make a point for each ordered pair below on the grid. Use line segments to connect the points in order. To draw a point, remember to follow the *x*-axis first and then the *y*-axis .

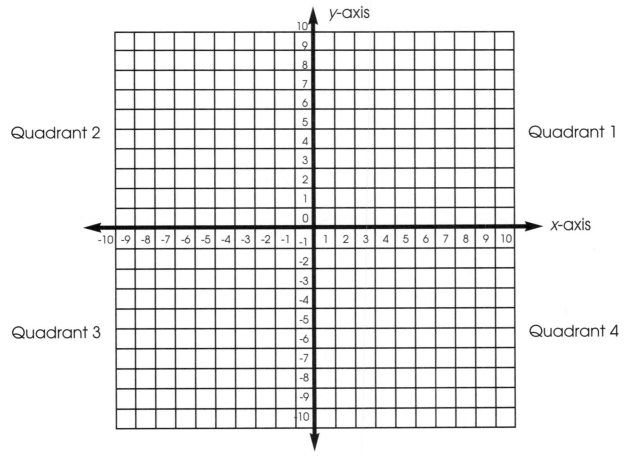

Quadrant 2

Quadrant 1

Quadrant 3

Quadrant 4

*y*-axis

*x*-axis

Main object: (0, 9), (2, 6) , (6, 4), (2, 2), (0, -9), (-2, 2), (-6, 4), (-2, 6), (0, 9)

Small objects:

(4, 6), (5, 9), (3, 8), (4, 6)          (-3, -3), (-2, -5), (-4, -6), (-3, -3)          (7, 3), (9, 4), (7, 5), (7, 3)

(-6, 1), (-5, -1), (-7, -2), (-6, 1)     (6, 1), (7, -2), (5, -1), (6, 1)          (-7, 3), (-7, 5), (-9, 4). (-7, 3)

(3, -3), (2, -5), (4, -6), (3, -3)       (-4, 6), (-3, 8), (-5, 9), (-4, 6)

Name _____

# Follow the Dots

| square | rectangle | parallelogram | rhombus | trapezoid |
|--------|-----------|---------------|---------|-----------|
| a rectangle with all sides congruent | a parallelogram with 4 right angles | opposite sides are parallel and congruent | a parallelogram with all sides congruent | only one set of parallel sides |

Use the ordered pairs to create quadrilaterals. Identify.

A.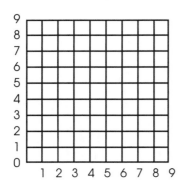

(3, 3), (6, 3), (6, 6), (3, 6)

_____

B.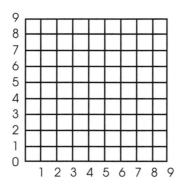

(1, 4), (6, 7), (8, 4), (3, 7)

_____

C.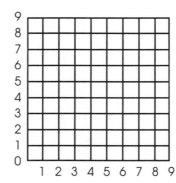

(6, 8), (2, 8), (6, 2), (2, 2)

_____

D.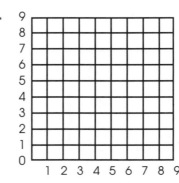

(8, 4), (9, 7), (3, 7), (2, 4)

_____

E.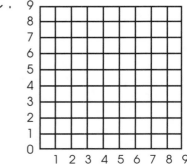

(1, 8), (5, 8), (4, 2), (8, 2)

_____

F.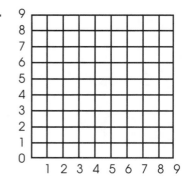

(4, 4), (9, 4), (6, 8), (1, 8)

_____

 On another piece of paper, draw a square, a rectangle, a parallelogram, a rhombus, and a trapezoid.

Name _____

# What Goes Around, Comes Around

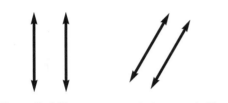

**Parallel lines** never intersect. They remain an equal distance apart.

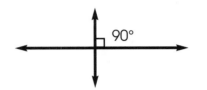

**Perpendicular lines** intersect creating a right angle.

Draw each polygon using the directions given. Name the polygon.

A. Draw a polygon with four equal sides of 3 cm and a right angle.

B. Draw a polygon with parallel sides and a right angle. Its length is 5 cm, and its width is 2 cm.

C. Draw a four-sided polygon with only two parallel sides. The top is 2 cm in length, and the bottom is 4 cm. The other two sides are 2 cm in length.

D. Draw a polygon with four sides. Opposite sides are parallel. The length of each side is 4 cm. No sides are perpendicular.

E. Draw a three-sided polygon. The lengths of two sides are 2 cm and 5 cm. The 2 cm and 5 cm sides are perpendicular and connect at a right angle. How long is the third side?

F. Draw a polygon with four sides. Opposite sides are parallel. Two of the opposite sides are 6 cm in length. The other two are 4 cm in length. No sides are perpendicular.

Name _____

# Face to Face

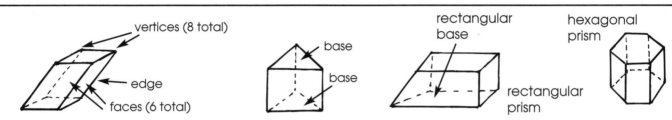

vertices (8 total)

edge

faces (6 total)

base

base

rectangular base

rectangular prism

hexagonal prism

Each face of a prism connects at an edge, and each edge connects at a vertex.

A prism has two bases that are congruent.

The name of a prism is determined by the polygons that make up its congruent bases.

Complete the chart. Write the name of each prism. Choose from these names: triangular, cube, rectangular, pentagonal, or hexagonal.

| | Type of prism | Name of prism | Number of faces | Number of edges | Number of vertices |
|---|---|---|---|---|---|
| A. | | | | | |
| B. | | | | | |
| C. | | | | | |
| D. | | | | | |
| E. | | | | | |

Name _____

# Egypt's Wonders

There are 6 sides. It is a hexagonal pyramid.

A pyramid has one base. The polygon that makes up that base determines the name of the pyramid.

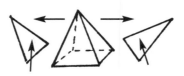

face          face

Each face is a triangle.

edge          vertex

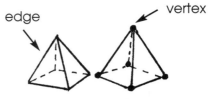

Each face of a pyramid connects at an edge. Each edge connects at a vertex.

Complete the chart. Write the name of each pyramid. Choose from these names: triangular, rectangular, pentagonal, or octagonal.

| | Type of pyramid | Name of pyramid | Number of faces (including the base) | Number of edges | Number of vertices |
|---|---|---|---|---|---|
| A. | | | | | |
| B. | | | | | |
| C. | | | | | |
| D. | | | | | |
| E. | | | | | |

Name _____

# Figure It Out

 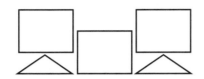 Prism check: Are there two congruent bases? Yes. Do the faces match and line up at the edge of the base? Yes.

Pyramid check: Is there only one base? Yes. Are the faces all triangles? Yes. Are there more faces than needed? No.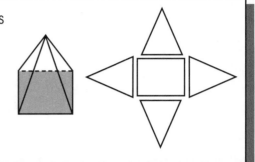

Check each diagram. If all the pieces are correct, draw the solid figure. If not, cross out the extra pieces. Then, draw.

A.

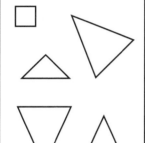   

B.

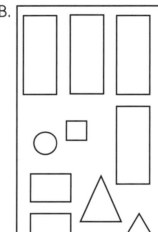 

C.

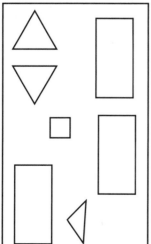

D.

Name _____

# Explore the Angle

To draw a 120° angle, follow these steps.

Draw the horizontal ray $\overrightarrow{XY}$.

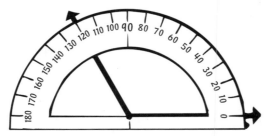

Line up the protractor. Make a point at 120°. Call it "point W."

Draw a ray from the vertex, point X, to form ∠WXY.

Draw each angle using a protractor.

| | | | |
|---|---|---|---|
| A. 70° | 90° | 20° | 50° |
| B. 80° | 110° | 40° | 60° |
| C. 150° | 35° | 130° | 145° |
| D. 10° | 175° | 100° | 95° |

Name _____

# What Type Am I?

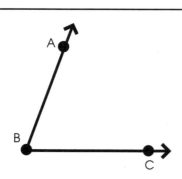

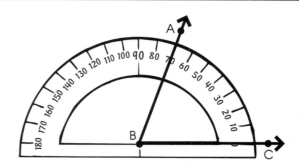

Two rays come together at a vertex to form an angle. Angle ABC is written as ∠ABC. The middle letter (B) is always the vertex of the angle.

A protractor is used to measure the degrees of an angle.
m∠ABC = 70°.

Measure the degrees of each angle using a protractor.

A.         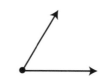   

_____    _____    _____    _____

B. 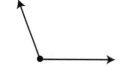    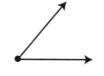    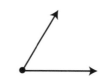   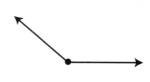

_____    _____    _____    _____

Measure each angle from the marked vertex. Identify the triangle as either **acute**, **right**, or **obtuse**. (acute = less than 90°, right = 90°, obtuse = greater than 90°)

C.         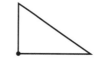   

_____    _____    _____    _____

D. 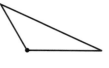           

_____    _____    _____    _____

Name _____

# Dreaming of Shapes

 An object can **slide** into a new position. (translation)

 An object can **flip** completely over. (reflection)

 An object can **turn** around a point. (rotation)

Identify as either a **slide**, **flip**, or **turn**.

A.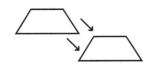

_____  _____  _____  _____

B.

_____  _____  _____  _____

C.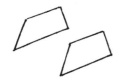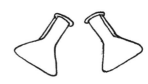

_____  _____  _____  _____

D.

_____  _____  _____  _____

E.

_____  _____  _____  _____

Similar and congruent

# Little Creatures

△ △

Objects that are the same shape but not the same size are said to be **similar**.

Objects that are the same size and shape are said to be **congruent**.

Draw a line to connect objects that look alike. Write **S** on the objects if they are similar. Write **C** on the objects if they are congruent.

Name _____

# How Far Is It?

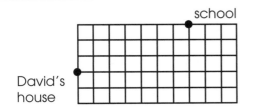

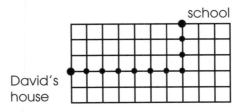

To travel from one block to the next is 0.5 miles. How far is it from school to David's home taking the shortest path?

The path you take determines the distance. What is the shortest path? Is there more than one path to take from David's house to school?

To determine a path's distance, count the blocks traveled to reach the location. The path using the fewest blocks is the path with the shortest distance. The shortest distance from David's house to school is 5 miles. Often there are several paths of equal distance.

Use each diagram to solve.

A. How far is it from the bicycle shop to the toy store taking the shortest route?

B. What is the distance from Eva's house to the school by way of Gwen's house?

C. Draw the shortest route from City Hall to the library. What is the distance?

_____

_____

_____

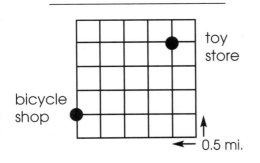

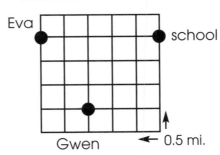

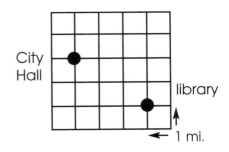

D. Draw three paths from Skate Park to Earl's house to Mark's tree fort. How far is the shortest route? _____

E. Draw a route from the movie theater to Kite Park by way of Martha and Andy's houses. What is the distance? _____

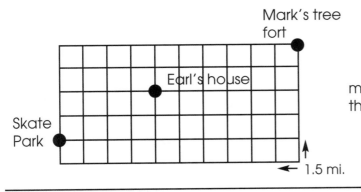

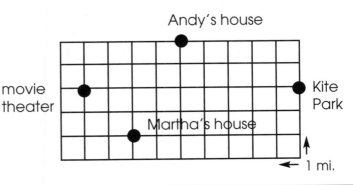

Name _____

# Mail Delivery

The mail carrier has to deliver to each of the "dots" along the path. Show how the mail carrier can deliver without crossing over the same path twice.

Place a •—► where you start. Write **end** where you finish. Use a colored pencil to show the path to take.

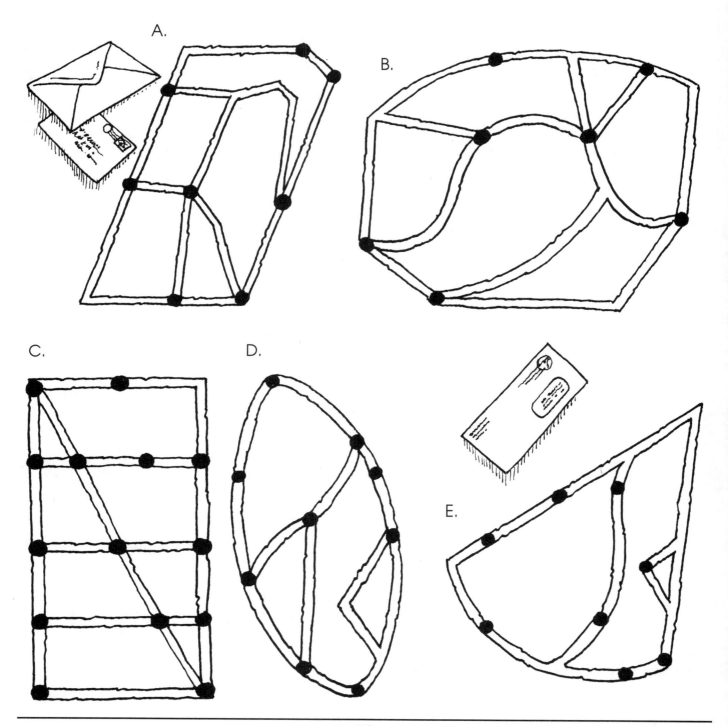

A.

B.

C.

D.

E.

Name _____

Line and rotational symmetry

# Identical Parts

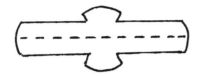

When an imaginary line divides a figure into two exactly identical parts, it is called a **line of symmetry**.

When a figure can turn less than a full turn and still be the same, it is said to possess **rotational symmetry**.

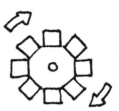

Circle yes or no to tell if the dotted line in each figure is a line of symmetry.

A.

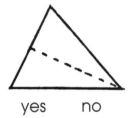

yes    no

B.

yes    no

C.

yes    no

D.

yes    no

Draw a line of symmetry in each figure.

E.

F.

G.

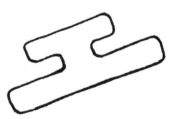

H.

I.

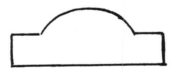

J.

Circle yes or no to tell if the figure possesses rotational symmetry.

K.

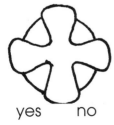

yes    no

L.

yes    no

M.

yes    no

N.

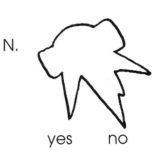

yes    no

Name _____

# From Your Perspective

Front view of object

3-D view of object

Top view of object

Letter to match objects.

**Top View**  **Side View**

A.

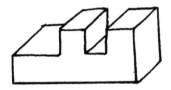

___   ___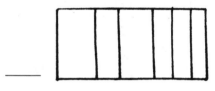

B.

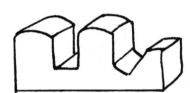

___ 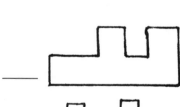  ___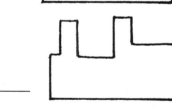

C.

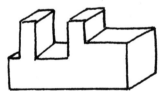

___ 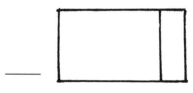  ___ (side view)

D.

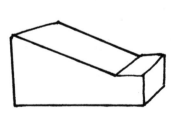

___ 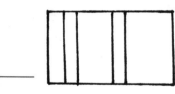  ___ (side view)

E. Draw the front and top view of the object.

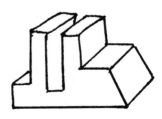

**Front View**  **Top View**

Name _____

# Added Dimensions

The **perimeter** of a polygon is the distance around the object.

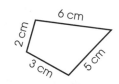

2 cm + 3 cm + 5 cm + 6 cm = 16 cm

Find the perimeter of each polygon.

A.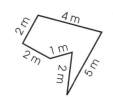
6 in.
2 in.

P = _____

B.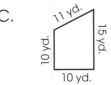
4 m
2 m
1 m
2 m
2 m
5 m

P = _____

C.
11 yd.
15 yd.
10 yd.
10 yd.

P = _____

D.
28 cm
10 cm    10 cm
8 cm    8 cm
8 cm    8 cm
10 cm

P = _____

E.
4 m
2.9 m
3 m
5.3 m
10.6 m
7.3 m

P = _____

F.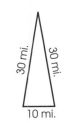
5 cm  7 cm
12 cm
15 cm
2 cm

P = _____

G.
30 mi.  30 mi.
10 mi.

P = _____

H.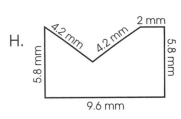
4.2 mm   4.2 mm   2 mm
5.8 mm            5.8 mm
9.6 mm

P = _____

Circle the best unit of measurement to find each perimeter.

I. around a school    in.   ft.   yd.   mi.

J. around a city    in.   ft.   yd.   mi.

K. around a classroom    in.   ft.   yd.   mi.

L. around a math book    in.   ft.   yd.   mi.

M. around a house    mm   cm   m   km

N. around a zoo    mm   cm   m   km

O. around a computer screen    mm   cm   m   km

P. around a keyboard    mm   cm   m   km

Q. around one key on a key pad    mm   cm   m   km

Name _____

# All Boxed In

The **area** of a figure is the number of square units in the figure.

To find the area of a square, multiply a side by a side.

$A = s \times s$
$A = 4 \times 4$
$A = 16 \text{ mm}^2$

4 mm

To find the area of a rectangle, multiply the length by the width.

$A = l \times w$
$A = 8 \times 4$
$A = 32 \text{ cm}^2$

8 cm
4 cm

Find the area.

A. 
10 m
4 m

$A =$ _____

B.
3 in.
12 in.

$A =$ _____

C.
2 ft.

$A =$ _____

D.
11 in.
7 in.

$A =$ _____

E.
8 cm
4 cm

$A =$ _____

F.
6 ft.
7 ft.

$A =$ _____

G.
5 mm

$A =$ _____

H.
10 mi.
12 mi.

$A =$ _____

I.
12 cm
3 cm

$A =$ _____

J.
5.4 m

$A =$ _____

K.
7.2 in.
3.5 in.

$A =$ _____

L.
4 ft.
8 ft.

$A =$ _____

 Find the area minus the rectangular holes.

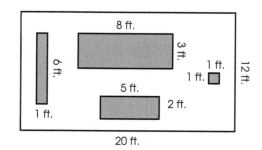

8 ft.
3 ft.
6 ft.
1 ft.
1 ft.
5 ft.
2 ft.
1 ft.
12 ft.
20 ft.

Area of right triangles

Name _____

# Triangular Designs

 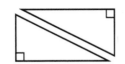

A **right triangle** is one-half of a rectangle in area. If a diagonal is drawn inside a rectangle, two right triangles are created.

A right triangle has one right angle.

The formula to find the area of a right triangle is
$A = 1/2(b \times h)$.

$A = 1/2(b \times h)$
$= 1/2(2 \times 8)$
$= 1/2(16)$
$= 8 \text{ cm}^2$

Figure the area of each right triangle.

A.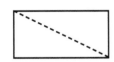

8 cm

6 cm

$A =$ _____

B.

8 ft.

2 ft.

$A =$ _____

C.

8 m

5.5 m

$A =$ _____

D.

3.5 in.

15 in.

$A =$ _____

E.

1.8 mm

6.4 mm

$A =$ _____

F.

3.5 ft.

1.5 ft.

$A =$ _____

G.

4 in.

16 in.

$A =$ _____

H.

10 cm

6.8 cm

$A =$ _____

Find the area minus the right triangle.

I.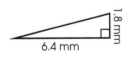

6 m

2 m

10 m

$A =$ _____

J.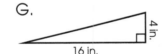

15 cm

6 cm

3 cm

2 cm

$A =$ _____

K.

8 in.

4 in.

12 in.

$A =$ _____

L.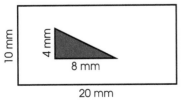

10 mm

4 mm

8 mm

20 mm

$A =$ _____

M.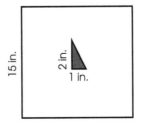

15 in.

2 in.

1 in.

$A =$ _____

N.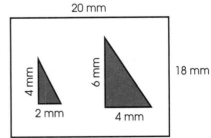

20 mm

4 mm

6 mm

2 mm

4 mm

18 mm

$A =$ _____

Name _____

# Figure This!

The formula for finding the area of a parallelogram is $A = b \times h$.

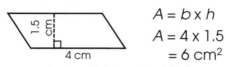

$A = b \times h$
$A = 4 \times 1.5$
$= 6 \text{ cm}^2$

Find the area of each parallelogram.

A.

2 cm
8.2 cm

$A = $ _____

B.

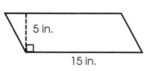

5 in.
15 in.

$A = $ _____

C.

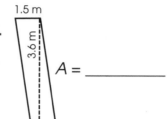

1.5 m
3.6 m

$A = $ _____

D.

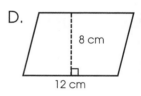

8 cm
12 cm

$A = $ _____

E.

3.2 ft.
7 ft.

$A = $ _____

F.

7 ft.
4.6 ft.

$A = $ _____

G.

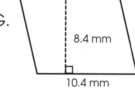

8.4 mm
10.4 mm

$A = $ _____

H.

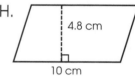

4.8 cm
10 cm

$A = $ _____

Find the area of each rectangle. (Hint: Each rectangle contains 1 parallelogram and 2 right triangles.)

I.

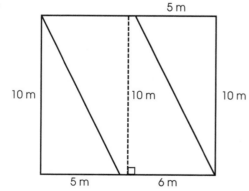

5 m
10 m    10 m    10 m
5 m    6 m

$A = $ _____

J.

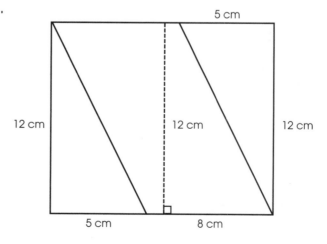

5 cm
12 cm    12 cm    12 cm
5 cm    8 cm

$A = $ _____

Name _____

# After School Activities

| perimeter of a figure: | area of a square: | area of a rectangle: | area of a right triangle: |
|---|---|---|---|
| $P$ = all sides added together. | $A = s^2$ | $A = l \times w$ | $A = 1/2(b \times h)$ |

Choose the formula. Solve each problem. Circle whether you are finding the perimeter or area.

A. Maria wants to paint her canvas background red. The dimensions are 4 ft. x 4 ft.

The formula: _____

The perimeter or area: _____

B. Mark wants to carpet the floor of his dog's house. The floor of Spot's doghouse has the dimensions 4 ft. x 6 ft.

The formula: _____  The perimeter or area: _____

C. Latosha wants to add some beautiful gold lace around the outside of her pillowcase. The length of the case is 2.5 ft., and the width is 1.5 ft.

The formula: _____  The perimeter or area: _____

D. Jonathan wants to know the distance around the playground. He runs it every week. The width of the field is 75 m, and the length is 150 m.

The formula: _____  The perimeter or area: _____

E. Earl has a small space of the yard to rake. It is in the shape of a right triangle and the dimensions are 12 ft. (base) x 25 ft. How large is the space Earl has to rake?

The formula: _____  The perimeter or area: _____

F. David's slice of pizza looks pretty good! He wants to figure out the area of the slice before he finds out how good it really is. It is cut at a perfect diagonal, and the bottom is a 90 degree angle. The base is 15 cm, and the height is 22 cm.

The formula: _____  The perimeter or area: _____

G. The dimensions of the school garden are 2 m x 6 m. How many square meter plots will there be to plant?

The formula: _____  The perimeter or area: _____

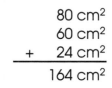

Name _____

# Spray Painting

Follow the steps to find the surface area of rectangular prisms.

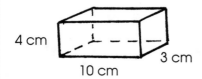

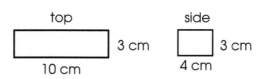

$$80 \text{ cm}^2$$
$$60 \text{ cm}^2$$
$$+ \quad 24 \text{ cm}^2$$
$$164 \text{ cm}^2$$

First, find the area of one face. ($4 \times 10 = 40 \text{ cm}^2$) There are two faces with the same area. Multiply by 2. ($2 \times 40 = 80 \text{ cm}^2$)

Next, find the area of the other four faces. Multiply each by 2. $3 \times 10 = 30 \text{ cm}^2$, $2 \times 30 = 60 \text{ cm}^2$ $3 \times 4 = 12 \text{ cm}^2$, $2 \times 12 = 24 \text{ cm}^2$

Then, add all the face areas. Surface area = $164 \text{ cm}^2$.

Andy is spray painting the following figures. Help him find the surface area of each figure.

A.
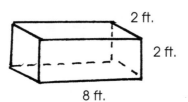

Surface Area = _____

B.
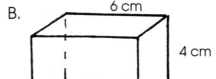

Surface Area = _____

C.
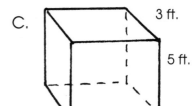

Surface Area = _____

D.
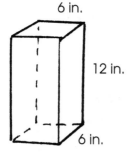

Surface Area = _____

E.
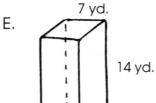

Surface Area = _____

F.
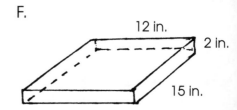

Surface Area = _____

G.
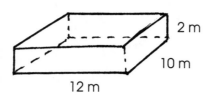

Surface Area = _____

H.
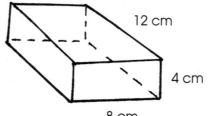

Surface Area = _____

Volume of rectangular prisms

# It Speaks Volumes

The volume of a figure is the number of cubic units of space inside the figure.

To find the volume, multiply the length times the width times the height.

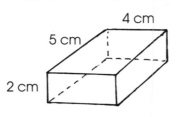

4 cm
5 cm
2 cm

$V = l \times w \times h$
$V = 5 \times 4 \times 2$
$V = 40 \text{ cm}^3$

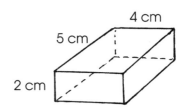

4 cm
5 cm
2 cm

There are 40 cubic centimeters inside this figure.

Find the volume of each figure.

A.

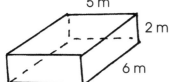

5 m
2 m
6 m

$V =$ _____

B.

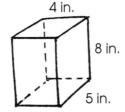

4 in.
8 in.
5 in.

$V =$ _____

C.

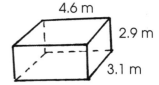

4.6 m
2.9 m
3.1 m

$V =$ _____

D.

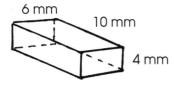

6 mm
10 mm
4 mm

$V =$ _____

E.

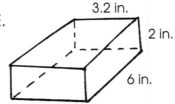

3.2 in.
2 in.
6 in.

$V =$ _____

F.

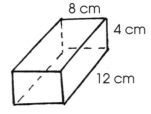

8 cm
4 cm
12 cm

$V =$ _____

G.

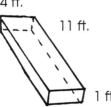

4 ft.
11 ft.
1 ft.

$V =$ _____

H.

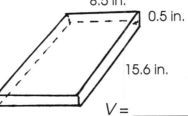

8.5 in.
0.5 in.
15.6 in.

$V =$ _____

Is 350 cubic feet of air enough to fill this model of a building? _____
Figure the total volume to find out.

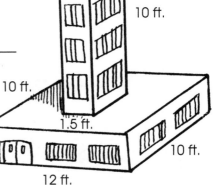

2 ft.
10 ft.
10 ft.
1.5 ft.
2 ft.
10 ft.
12 ft.

Name _____

# A Good Yarn

The **circumference** is the distance around a circle.

The **diameter** is a line segment that goes from one edge of a circle to the other edge intersecting the center.

5 cm

$\pi \approx 3.14$ (pi)
$d = 5$ cm

15.7 cm

The formula:
$C = \pi \times d$
$C \approx 3.14 \times 5$ cm
$C \approx 15.7$ cm

$\pi$ is the ratio of the circumference of a circle to its diameter.
$\pi$ is approximately equal to 3.14.

Monica has started several art projects. Her designs require a lot of yarn. If each circle is made with yarn, what will be the total amount of yarn used for each design? To find the total for each design, find the circumference for each circle. Then add.

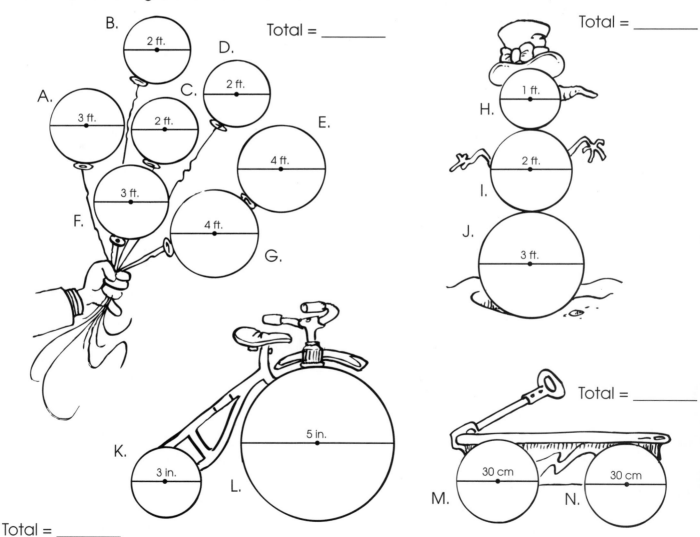

B.
2 ft.

Total = _____

D.
2 ft.

A.
3 ft.

C.
2 ft.

E.
4 ft.

F.
3 ft.

G.
4 ft.

Total = _____

H.
1 ft.

I.
2 ft.

J.
3 ft.

K.
3 in.

5 in.

L.

Total = _____

M.
30 cm

N.
30 cm

Total = _____

Name _____

# Bubble Mania

The **area** of a circle is the number of square units needed to cover the circle.

The **radius** is a line segment that extends from the center of a circle to the outer edge.

radius

The formula:

$A = \pi r^2$

$\pi \approx 3.14$

$r = 2$ cm

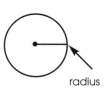
2 cm

Area:

$A = 3.14 \times 2^2$

$A = 3.14 \times 4$

$A = 12.56$ cm$^2$

Find the area of each circle.

A.

10 m

A = _____

B.
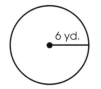
6 yd.

A = _____

C.

9 m

A = _____

D.

8 mm

A = _____

E.

3 cm

A = _____

F.

1 m

A = _____

G.
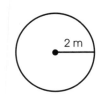
2 m

A = _____

H.

5 yd.

A = _____

I.
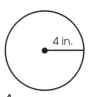
4 in.

A = _____

J.
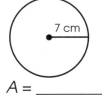
7 cm

A = _____

What is the area of the rectangle without the large hole? Hint: Find the circle area and then subtract it from the area of the rectangle.

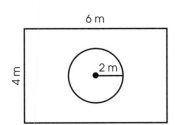
6 m
4 m
2 m

Name _____

# Simply Cylinders

The **surface area** of a spatial figure is the combined area of the figure's outer surfaces. To find the surface area of a cylinder, follow the example below.

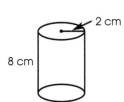

2 cm

8 cm

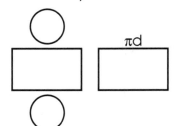

πd

There are two circles and a rectangle that make up the surface of a cylinder.

The cylinder uncurls to form a rectangle. The width of the rectangle is the circumference of one of the circles.

area of cylinder's rectangle:

= π*d* x *h*
≈ 3.14 x 4 x 8
≈ 100.48 cm²

area of one flat circle face:

= π*r*²
= 3.14 x 2 x 2
= 12.56 cm²

To find the surface area of the cylinder, add together each face.
100.48 cm² + 12.56 cm² + 12.56 cm²

Find the surface area of each cylinder.

A.

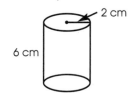

2 cm

6 cm

Surface area: _____

B.

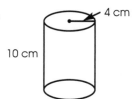

4 cm

10 cm

Surface area: _____

C.

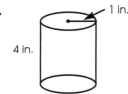

1 in.

4 in.

Surface area: _____

D.

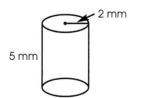

2 mm

5 mm

Surface area: _____

E.

3 ft.

8 ft.

Surface area: _____

F.

3 cm

7 cm

Surface area: _____

G.

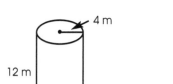

4 in.

4 in.

Surface area: _____

H.

4 m

12 m

Surface area: _____

I.

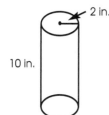

2 in.

10 in.

Surface area: _____

Name _____

# Heavyweight

| 16 oz. = 1 lb. |
| 2,000 lb. = 1 ton |
| 2 c. = 1 pt. |
| 2 pt. = 1 qt. |
| 4 qt. = 1 gal. |

Convert each customary unit of weight.

A. 32 oz. = _____ lb.        3 lb. = _____ oz.

B. 8 oz. = _____ lb.        4 oz. = _____ lb.

C. 1 ton = _____ lb.        4,000 lb. = _____ tons

D. 80 oz. = _____ lb.        6 lb. = _____ oz.

Convert each customary unit of capacity.

E. 2 c. = _____ pt.        3 pt. = _____ c.        6 c. = _____ pt.        2 pt. = _____ qt.

F. 4 qt. = _____ gal.        4 pt. = _____ qt.        8 qt. = _____ gal.        8 pt. = _____ gal.

G. 1 qt. = _____ gal.        1 pt. = _____ qt.        1 cup = _____ gal.        1 pt. = _____ gal.

Write the correct unit of measurement. Choose **cups**, **pints**, **quarts**, or **gallons**.

H. filling up a gas tank _____

I. donating blood _____

J. drinking tea _____

K. buying large plastic jugs of milk _____

L. four equal parts of one gallon of ice cream _____

M. the capacity of a fish tank _____

N. measuring flour for a recipe _____

Name _____

# Go the Extra Mile

| 12 in. = 1 ft. |
| 3 ft. = 1 yd. |
| 5,280 ft. = 1 mi. |
| 1,760 yd. = 1 mi. |

Convert each customary unit of length.

A. 12 in. = _____ ft.          18 in. = _____ ft.          2 ft. = _____ in.

B. 48 in. = _____ ft.          6 ft. = _____ yd.          7 yd. = _____ ft.

C. 1 yd. = _____ in.          9 ft. = _____ yd.          3 yd. = _____ ft.

D. 6 in. = _____ ft.          10 yd. = _____ ft.          11 ft. = _____ in.

Subtract.

E.      15 yd.  4 ft.      F.      32 ft.  9 in.      G.      35 yd.  1 ft.      H.      1 ft.  5 in.
    –    8 yd.  3 ft.          –  12 ft.  6 in.          –  12 yd.  2 ft.          –          9 in.

Choose the correct unit of measurement. Choose **miles**, **yards**, **feet**, or **inches**.

I. the distance from your house to the airport _____

J. the distance from your bedroom to the kitchen _____

K. the length of a dining room table _____

L. the length of your pencil _____

M. the length of a playground or soccer field _____

Measure each using a standard ruler.

N. ▬▬▬▬▬▬▬▬▬▬▬▬                    _____

O. ▬▬▬▬▬▬                    _____

P. ▬▬▬▬▬▬▬▬▬                    _____

Name _____

# The "Eyes" Have It

| millimeters (mm) | 10 mm = 1 cm |
| centimeters (cm) | 10 cm = 1 dm |
| decimeters (dm) | 10 dm = 1 m |
| meters (m) | 1,000 mm or 100 cm = 1 m |
| kilometers (km) | 1,000 m = 1 km |

Convert.

A. 20 mm = _____ cm      3 cm = _____ mm      30 cm = _____ dm

B. 5 dm = _____ cm       7 dm = _____ cm      90 cm = _____ dm

C. 30 dm = _____ m       2m = _____ dm        1,000 mm = _____m

Write the correct unit of measurement. Choose millimeters (**mm**), centimeters (**cm**), decimeters (**dm**), meters (**m**), or kilometers (**km**).

D. the width of a grasshopper _____

E. the width of a book _____

F. the distance from the classroom door to your desk _____

G. the distance from your front door to the school _____

H. the length of your pencil _____

**Why don't fish blink?** To find out, measure the perimeter of each shape in millimeters. Match each perimeter to a word in the key. Then, write the word under each shape.

| **Key** |
| 70 mm = never |
| 50 mm = their |
| 100 mm = become |
| 80 mm = eyes |
| 75 mm = dry |

_____   _____   _____

_____   _____.

Name _____

# Mass and Volume

Liquid unit conversions

1 L = 1,000 mL

1 kL = 1,000 L

1 cubic cm = 1 mL

 1 L

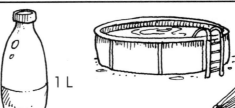

1 kL — about 250 gallons

Mass unit conversions

1 g = 1,000 mg

1 kg = 1,000 g

 1 mg

1 g

1 kg

Convert.

A. 1,000 mL = _____ L         1,000 L = _____ kL         4 L = _____ mL

B. 5 kL = _____ L             3,000 mL = _____ L         9 L = _____ mL

C. 8 kL = _____ L             2,000 L = _____ kL         4 g = _____ mg

Write the correct unit of measurement. Choose milliliters (**mL**), liters (**L**), kiloliters (**kL**), milligrams (**mg**), grams (**g**), or kilograms (**kg**).

D. the capacity of a pitcher of orange juice _____

E. the capacity of water in a swimming pool _____

F. the mass of a gecko _____

G. the mass of a Great Dane _____

H. the mass of a watermelon seed _____

**Why do flies buzz and not chirp?** To find out, convert each measurement to one found in the Key. Then, write the word on the line.

| **Key** | |
|---|---|
| and = 8L | too = 5,000 mL |
| is = 4 g | chirping = 11 kL |
| the = 3 g | crickets = 2,000 L |
| for = 9 kg | birds = 7,000 mg |
| ! = 6,000 g | |

_____ _____ _____ _____ _____
11,000 L   4,000 mg   9,000 g   3,000 mg   7 g

_____ _____, _____ _____
8,000 mL   2 kL   5 L   6 kg

Name _____

# Let's Compare!

| | | |
|---|---|---|
| 1 ft. = 30.5 cm | 1 qt. ≈ 0.945 L | 1 lb. ≈ 454 g |
| 3 ft. = 91.5 cm | 1 gal. ≈ 3.78 L | 2 lb. ≈ 908 g |
| 1 yd. = 91.5 cm | | |
| 1 mi. = 1,610.4 m | | |
| 1 mi. = 1.6 km | | |

Compare using **<**, **>**, or **=**.

A.  3 ft. ◯ 1 m          1 mi. ◯ 1 km          3 yd. ◯ 1 m          1 mi. ◯ 1.6 km

B.  1 m ◯ 1 yd.          91.5 cm ◯ 1 yd.          1 qt. ◯ 1 L          1 gal. ◯ 4 L

C.  4 qt. ◯ 4 L          3 L ◯ 1 gal.          1 L ◯ 1 qt.          2 lb. ◯ 1 kg

D.  2 kg ◯ 2 lb.          500 g ◯ 1 lb.          3 km ◯ 2 mi.          1 kg ◯ 3 lb.

Circle the measurement that is greater.

E.  3 ft.     1 m          F.  2 m     8 ft.          G.  1 mi.     1 km          H.  1 km     3 ft.

I.  1 yd.     1 m          J.  4 ft.     1 m          K.  1 qt.     1 L          L.  3 gal.     3 L

M.  5 L     1 qt.          N.  3 lb.     500 g          O.  1 kg     2 lb.          P.  1 lb.     1 mg

Circle the better deal.

Q.  6 ft. of rope

    2 m of rope

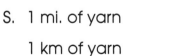

R.  1 gal. of olive oil

    8 L of olive oil

S.  1 mi. of yarn

    1 km of yarn

T.  5 lb. of potatoes

    5 kg of potatoes

Name _____

# Degrees Fahrenheit

Degrees **Fahrenheit** (°F) are U.S. customary units of measurement. The thermometer to the right displays the more common readings of temperatures and what these mean to us.

room temperature 68° F

212° F Water boils.

normal body temperature 98.6° F

32° F Water freezes.

Write the temperature. Then, write **BT** (normal body temperature), **RT** (normal room temperature), **BP** (the boiling point for water), or **FP** (the freezing point for water) on the line below the correct thermometer.

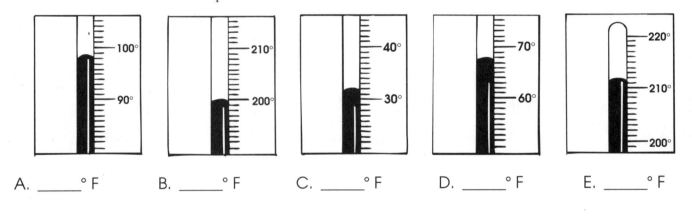

A. _____° F

B. _____° F

C. _____° F

D. _____° F

E. _____° F

_____   _____   _____   _____   _____

Tell what will happen.

F. The temperature is 127° F. The temperature rises 85°. There is a pan of water in the room. _____
Temperature: _____° F

G. The temperature is 59° F. The temperature drops 27°. There is a glass of water in the room. _____
Temperature: _____° F

H. You are outside building a snowman. The temperature is 29° F. The sun comes out, and the temperature rises 15°. _____
Temperature: _____° F

Name _____

# Degrees Celsius

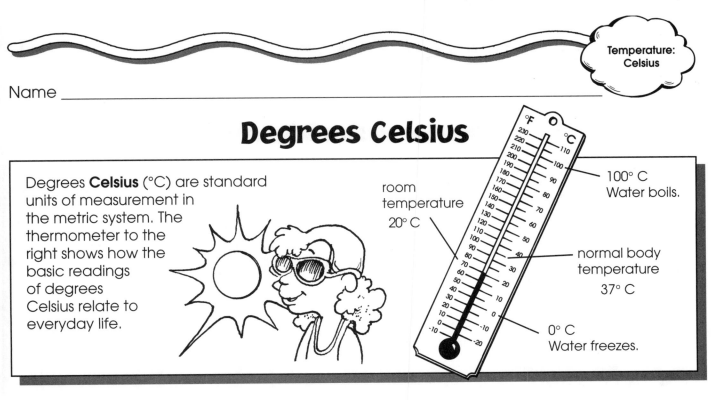

Degrees **Celsius** (°C) are standard units of measurement in the metric system. The thermometer to the right shows how the basic readings of degrees Celsius relate to everyday life.

room temperature
20° C

100° C
Water boils.

normal body temperature
37° C

0° C
Water freezes.

Write the temperature. Then, write **BT** (normal body temperature), **RT** (normal room temperature), **BP** (the boiling point for water), or **FP** (the freezing point for water) on the line below the correct thermometer.

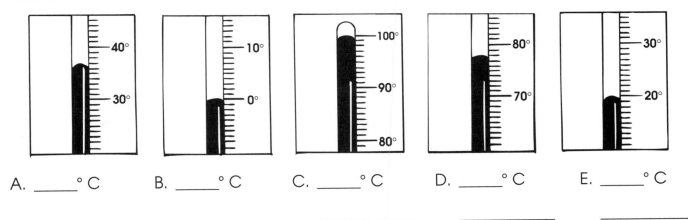

A. _____° C

B. _____° C

C. _____° C

D. _____° C

E. _____° C

_____

_____

_____

Determine each new temperature. Start at the beginning temperature each time.

F. Begins at 0° C.

Rises 40°. _____° C          Drops 20°. _____° C          Rises 70°. _____° C

G. Begins at 100° C.

Rises 25°. _____° C          Drops 63°. _____° C          Rises 4°. _____° C

What would you wear—a jacket or T-shirt?          What would you like—a hot or cold drink?

H. 40° C _____          J. 37° C _____

I. 0° C _____          K. -10° C _____

Name _____

# Let's Check Our Calendar

Use the calendars to answer the questions.

A. What is the date three weeks after the first Wednesday in April? _____

B. What is the date of the second Friday in April?

_____

C. What day comes 12 days after April 14?

_____

D. What day comes three days after April 7?

_____

E. What day falls four days before April 9?

_____

F. Is it possible to meet five Friday mornings for choir rehearsal in April? _____

### April

| S | M | T | W | T | F | S |
|---|---|---|---|---|---|---|
|   |   |   |   | 1 | 2 | 3 |
| 4 | 5 | 6 | 7 | 8 | 9 | 10 |
| 11 | 12 | 13 | 14 | 15 | 16 | 17 |
| 18 | 19 | 20 | 21 | 22 | 23 | 24 |
| 25 | 26 | 27 | 28 | 29 | 30 |   |

### January

| S | M | T | W | T | F | S |
|---|---|---|---|---|---|---|
| 1 | 2 | 3 | 4 | 5 | 6 | 7 |
| 8 | 9 | 10 | 11 | 12 | 13 | 14 |
| 15 | 16 | 17 | 18 | 19 | 20 | 21 |
| 22 | 23 | 24 | 25 | 26 | 27 | 28 |
| 29 | 30 | 31 |   |   |   |   |

G. On what day does January 24 fall?

_____

H. How many days are between Monday, January 9, and Saturday, January 14?

_____

I. How many weeks are between Monday, January 2, and Tuesday, January 17?

_____

J. Are there at least three full weeks remaining in January after Thursday, January 5?

_____

K. What is the date of the last Thursday in January? _____

Name _____

# Where Did the Time Go?

60 seconds (sec.) = 1 minute
60 minutes (min.) = 1 hour
24 hours (hr.) = 1 day
7 days (d.) = 1 week
52 weeks (wk.) = 1 year (yr.)
12 months (mo.) = 1 year
10 years = 1 decade
100 years = 1 century
1,000 years = 1 millennium

Andy started his project at 8:23 A.M.
He finished at 12:35 P.M. To find the
elapsed time, subtract.

```
   12:35        12 hr. 35 min.
 -  8:23      -  8 hr. 23 min.
              ─────────────────
                 4 hr. 12 min.
```

It took a total of 4 hours and 12 minutes.

Solve.

A. Otis and Albert started their skateboard journey at 7:39 A.M. They zoomed around town and finished back at their house at 11:56 A.M., just in time for lunch. How long did their journey take? _____

B. Craig and Sing Lee love to listen to birds sing in the morning. They met at 7:59 A.M. and sat on the swings at school to listen to the birds until the bell rang. If the bell rang 26 minutes later, what time did the bell ring to go in and start school? _____

C. David and Eva timed how long it took their plants to germinate and then bloom with beautiful flowers. It took 24 days and 22 hours. Miguel and Anita also timed their plants' growth. Their plants took 17 days and 14 hours. What was the difference in time? _____

D. The carnival began in the morning at the time shown on the clock.

1. Two hours after the carnival began, Alecia took a break and got a drink. What time did she take a break? _____

2. Four hours and 22 minutes after the carnival began, Monica had to go home. What time did she leave for home?

    _____

E. We arrived at the beach in the early afternoon at the time shown on the clock.

1. The girls finished their sandcastle 1 hour and 25 minutes after they arrived. What time did they finish the castle? _____

2. Two hours after arriving, the boys stopped swimming to play football on the beach. What time did they start playing football? _____

Name _____

# Clocking Our Fun Time

| Begin by adding the minutes. | Convert and regroup. (60 min. = 1 hr.) | Add the hours. |
|---|---|---|
| 3 hr. 45 min. <br> + 2 hr. 20 min. <br> 65 min. | ¹3 hr. 45 min. <br> + 2 hr. 20 min. <br> 5 min. | 3 hr. 45 min. <br> + 2 hr. 20 min. <br> 6 hr. 5 min. |

| Begin by subtracting the minutes. Borrow, convert, and regroup. (1 hr. = 60 min.) | Subtract the hours. |
|---|---|
| 7    70 <br> 8̶ hr. 1̶0̶ min. <br> – 2 hr. 35 min. <br> 35 min. | 7    70 <br> 8̶ hr. 1̶0̶ min. <br> – 2 hr. 35 min. <br> 5 hr. 35 min. |

## Add.

A.
$$
\begin{array}{r}
3\text{ hr. } 25\text{ min.} \\
+\ 8\text{ hr. } 14\text{ min.} \\
\hline
\end{array}
\qquad
\begin{array}{r}
10\text{ hr. } 42\text{ min.} \\
+\ 8\text{ hr. } 34\text{ min.} \\
\hline
\end{array}
\qquad
\begin{array}{r}
22\text{ min. } 18\text{ sec.} \\
+\ 32\text{ min. } 29\text{ sec.} \\
\hline
\end{array}
$$

B.
$$
\begin{array}{r}
3\text{ d. } 13\text{ hr.} \\
+\ 2\text{ d. } 22\text{ hr.} \\
\hline
\end{array}
\qquad
\begin{array}{r}
12\text{ hr. } 2\text{ min.} \\
+\ 3\text{ hr. } 59\text{ min.} \\
\hline
\end{array}
\qquad
\begin{array}{r}
2\text{ wk. } 3\text{ d.} \\
+\ 7\text{ wk. } 6\text{ d.} \\
\hline
\end{array}
$$

C.
$$
\begin{array}{r}
14\text{ d. } 15\text{ hr.} \\
+\ 3\text{ d. } 21\text{ hr.} \\
\hline
\end{array}
\qquad
\begin{array}{r}
13\text{ hr. } 21\text{ min.} \\
+\ 7\text{ hr. } 13\text{ min.} \\
\hline
\end{array}
\qquad
\begin{array}{r}
14\text{ wk. } 2\text{ d.} \\
+\ 3\text{ wk. } 5\text{ d.} \\
\hline
\end{array}
$$

## Subtract.

D.
$$
\begin{array}{r}
5\text{ hr. } 14\text{ min.} \\
-\ 2\text{ hr. } 20\text{ min.} \\
\hline
\end{array}
\qquad
\begin{array}{r}
15\text{ hr. } 29\text{ min.} \\
-\ 8\text{ hr. } 40\text{ min.} \\
\hline
\end{array}
\qquad
\begin{array}{r}
29\text{ min. } 25\text{ sec.} \\
-\ 14\text{ min. } 26\text{ sec.} \\
\hline
\end{array}
$$

E.
$$
\begin{array}{r}
3\text{ d. } 9\text{ hr.} \\
-\ 1\text{ d. } 12\text{ hr.} \\
\hline
\end{array}
\qquad
\begin{array}{r}
6\text{ wk. } 4\text{ d.} \\
-\ 2\text{ wk. } 6\text{ d.} \\
\hline
\end{array}
\qquad
\begin{array}{r}
21\text{ hr. } 15\text{ min.} \\
-\ 9\text{ hr. } 35\text{ min.} \\
\hline
\end{array}
$$

F.
$$
\begin{array}{r}
55\text{ min. } 29\text{ sec.} \\
-\ 21\text{ min. } 42\text{ sec.} \\
\hline
\end{array}
\qquad
\begin{array}{r}
31\text{ min. } 49\text{ sec.} \\
-\ 22\text{ min. } 38\text{ sec.} \\
\hline
\end{array}
\qquad
\begin{array}{r}
23\text{ hr. } 43\text{ min.} \\
-\ 18\text{ hr. } 51\text{ min.} \\
\hline
\end{array}
$$

Math Practice: Grades 5–6

Name _____

# Don't You Love It?

**Scattergrams** allow conclusions to be drawn about data in a very unique way. When comparing two different things that might have an effect upon each other, the data collected when placed on a scattergram shows if there is any relationship between them.

For example: Does spending more hours training a dog allow it to learn more tricks? Look at the possible results on the scattergram. Note how the dots rise as the hours spent training increases. According to the data collected, there is a positive correlation, or direct impact, on the hours spent training a dog and the amount that the dog learns!

**Tricks Learned vs. Hours in Training**

Answer the questions that relate to each scattergram below.

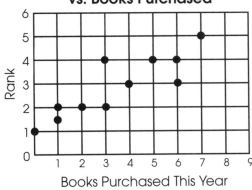

**Survey on the Love of Reading vs. Books Purchased**

A. Were many books purchased by those that only gave reading a rank of "1"? _____

B. Were there a lot of books purchased by those that gave reading a rank of "5"? _____

C. What might one conclude after looking at the results of this survey?

_____

_____

_____

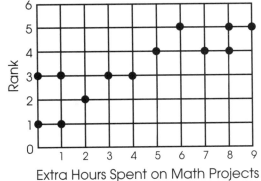

**Survey on the Love of Mathematics vs. Extra Hours Spent on Math Projects**

D. What is the relationship between love of math and extra hours spent on math projects? _____

_____

E. Where do you fit on this scattergram?

_____

F. If you loved or disliked mathematics more or less, would your response change? _____

_____

Name _____

# Can You Give Me the Time of Day?

| Hawaii-Aleutian Time | Alaska Standard Time | Pacific Time | Mountain Time | Central Time | Eastern Time |
|---|---|---|---|---|---|
| 4:00 P.M. | 5:00 P.M. | 6:00 P.M. | 7:00 P.M. | 8:00 P.M. | 9:00 P.M. |

Complete each chart. Pretend that you are on the phone. Tell the time it is for each person that you are talking to.

**A. You are calling from:**

| Sacramento, CA— Pacific Time | 5:00 P.M. |
|---|---|
| Dallas, TX— Central Time | |
| Juneau, AK— Alaska Standard Time | |
| Aspen, CO— Mountain Time | |

**B. You are calling from:**

| Miami, FL— Eastern Time | 10:00 P.M. |
|---|---|
| Fairbanks, AK— Alaska Standard Time | |
| Chicago, IL— Central Time | |
| Astoria, OR— Pacific Time | |

**C. You are calling from:**

| Honolulu, Hawaii— Hawaii-Aleutian Time | 7:00 A.M. |
|---|---|
| St. Louis, MO— Central Time | |
| Phoenix, AZ— Mountain Time | |
| Seattle, WA— Pacific Time | |

Now pretend you are flying! Complete the chart below using the time information above. Remember: if you are flying east, you add (+) time zones, if you are flying west, you subtract (–) time zones.

| | Departure Time Place of Departure | Flight Time | Direction | Time Zone Adjustment | Destination | Arrival Time |
|---|---|---|---|---|---|---|
| D. | 6:00 A.M. Los Angeles (Pacific Time) | 5 hr. | East | Add 3 hours. | New York (Eastern Time) | |
| E. | 1:00 A.M. Boston (Eastern Time) | 6 hr. 25 min. | West | | Los Angeles (Pacific Time) | |
| F. | 8:00 A.M. Phoenix (Mountain Time) | 3 hr. 10 min. | East | | Chicago (Central Time) | |
| G. | 12:00 noon Los Angeles (Pacific Time) | 3 hr. 28 min. | East | | St. Louis (Central Time) | |
| H. | 10:00 A.M. New York City (Eastern Time) | 6 hr. | West | | San Francisco (Pacific Time) | |

Name _____

# Ups and Downs

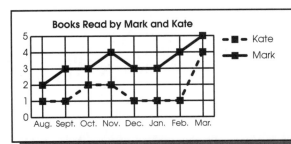

Line graphs are connected to show how data changes over time. Double line graphs compare two sets of data at the same time.

Use the line graphs below to answer each question.

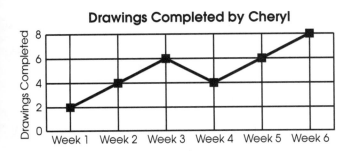

A. How many drawings did Cheryl complete the first week? _____

B. How many more drawings did she complete the third week than the first week? _____

C. How many drawings did Cheryl complete in all during the six-week period? _____

D. Did Thomas or Gwen practice the most on Sept. 1? _____

E. Did Thomas' practice time increase or decrease after Sept. 15? _____

F. How many more hours did Thomas practice on Sept. 28 than Gwen? _____

G. What day did they both practice the same number of hours? _____

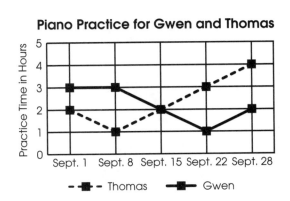

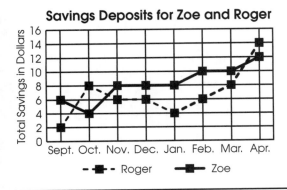

H. Did Zoe's pattern of saving increase or decrease after her deposit in Oct.? _____

I. Who deposited the most in the month of January? _____

J. What direction did Roger's deposits go after January? _____

Name _____

# "Chart" Your Course

Answer each question using the charts below.

## Thinking of Others Food Bank

| Donations | Year 1 | Year 2 | Year 3 | Year 4 |
|---|---|---|---|---|
| cans of tuna | 302 | 298 | 425 | 542 |
| bags of dry beans | 140 | 180 | 160 | 346 |
| boxes of spaghetti | 120 | 140 | 160 | 200 |
| pounds of fresh fruit | 500 | 300 | 500 | 600 |
| boxes of cereal | 25 | 149 | 275 | 291 |

A. Over the four-year period, what was the average cereal donation? _____

B. Which had a greater sum total of donations, bags of dry beans or pounds of fresh fruit? _____

C. What was the total poundage in fresh fruit donations? _____

D. What was the sum total of cans of tuna donated? _____

E. What was the average donation of boxes of spaghetti over the four-year period?

_____

## Animal Hut Store Sales for the Last Ten Years

| Animal | # Sold |
|---|---|
| puppies | 3,923 |
| kittens | 2,437 |
| birds | 1,429 |
| fish | 13,249 |
| reptiles | 1,211 |

G. Which type of animal had the greatest number of sales? _____

H. Round each animal category to the nearest thousand. What is the sum total? _____

I. What is the total number of puppies and kittens sold?

_____

J. How many more fish were sold than birds? _____

Name _____

# How Many Times?

Answer each question using the frequency tables below.

A. What is the range of sightings this year? (To find the range, subtract the least number of sightings from the greatest number.) _____

B. Which time period had the greatest number of sightings? _____

C. What was the average number of sightings? _____

D. Order the times in frequency from least to greatest.

_____  _____  _____  _____  _____

**Butterflies Sighted by Mr. Wong's Science Class**

| Time | Frequency |
|------|-----------|
| 8–9 A.M. | 22 |
| 9–10 A.M. | 55 |
| 10–11 A.M. | 72 |
| 11 A.M.–12 P.M. | 66 |
| 12–1 P.M. | 55 |

**School Lunch Favorites Ordered This Week**

| Type of Food | Frequency |
|--------------|-----------|
| pizza | 150 |
| spaghetti | 40 |
| lasagna | 80 |
| bean burrito | 75 |
| cheese crisp | 60 |
| tuna salad | 20 |

E. How many more times was pizza ordered than bean burritos? _____

F. How many more times was spaghetti ordered than tuna salad? _____

G. The sum total of which two foods is greater than the orders for pizza? _____

_____

H. What is the total number of lunches ordered this week? _____

I. When would be the best time to make sure the most volunteers were scheduled to help run the carnival? _____

J. What was the total number of people in attendance at the carnival? _____

K. What was the range of people in attendance? _____

**School Carnival Attendance**

| Time | Frequency |
|------|-----------|
| 9–10 A.M. | 56 |
| 10–11 A.M. | 75 |
| 11 A.M.–12 P.M. | 130 |
| 12–1 P.M. | 175 |
| 1–2 P.M. | 210 |

Name _____

# Lining Up Pictures

A **pictograph** displays quantities of information according to the value of each picture.

**Students Wearing Bicycle Helmets**

| Sept. | 🪖 🪖 🪖 🪖 | ← 4 x 10 = 40 helmets |
| Oct. | 🪖 🪖 | |
| Nov. | 🪖 🪖 🪖 | |
| Dec. | 🪖 🪖 🪖 🪖 🪖 | |

🪖 = 10 helmets   ⛑ = 5 helmets (1/2 of 10)

Answer each question using the pictographs.

**Roller Skates Sold**

| Week 1 | 🛼 🛼 |
| Week 2 | 🛼 🛼 🛼 🛼 🛼 |
| Week 3 | 🛼 🛼 🛼 🛼 |
| Week 4 | 🛼 🛼 🛼 🛼 🛼 🛼 🛼 |
| Week 5 | 🛼 |

🛼 = 4 pairs of roller skates sold

A. During which week were the most skates sold? _____

B. How many more pairs of skates were sold during week 4 than during week 5? _____

C. What was the total number of pairs of skates sold during this 5-week period? _____

D. Order each week's sales from least to greatest. ____ ____ ____ ____ ____

E. Which type of apple was the least favorite?
_____

F. What was the total number of votes for Gala and Golden Delicious? _____

G. How many more votes did Gala receive than Red Delicious? _____

H. What was the total number of votes cast?
_____

**Favorite Apples**

| Red Delicious | 🍎 🍎 🍎 🍎 |
| Granny Smith | 🍎 🍎 |
| Gala | 🍎 🍎 🍎 🍎 🍏 |
| Golden Delicious | 🍎 🍏 |

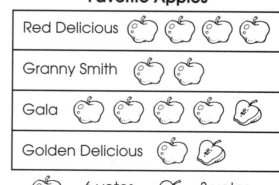

🍎 = 6 votes   🍏 = 3 votes

Name _____

# Fun at the Skating Park

Stem-and-leaf plots show a group of data. The stem is usually a tens digit, and the leaves are usually a ones digit. Look at this example:
21, 21, 21, 23, 23, 35, 40, 44, 44

| Stem | Leaf | |
|------|------|---|
| 0 | | |
| 1 | | |
| 2 | 1, 1, 1, 3, 3 | (21, 21, 21, 23, 23) |
| 3 | 5 | (35) |
| 4 | 0, 4, 4 | (40, 44, 44) |

Kids are enjoying the brand new skating park! Look at the number of boys and girls that have come each day since it opened: 13, 13, 18, 18, 18, 20, 23, 27, 31, 31, 35, 38, 40, 42, 46, 46. Place this data on the stem-and-leaf plot below.

**Attendance at Skating Park**

| Stem | Leaf |
|------|------|
| 0 | |
| 1 | |
| 2 | |
| 3 | |
| 4 | |

A. Which number occurs most often? _____

B. What is the least number of boys and girls that came? _____

C. What is the greatest number? _____

D. How often did the greatest number occur? _____

David and Eva have been keeping track of hot dog sales at their softball park refreshment stand. Here is the data: 12, 12, 13, 17, 21, 22, 22, 22, 22, 30, 32, 37. Place this data on the stem-and-leaf plot below.

**Hot Dog Sales**

| Stem | Leaf |
|------|------|
| 0 | |
| 1 | |
| 2 | |
| 3 | |

E. What is the least number of hot dogs sold on a given night? _____

F. On the best night, how many hot dogs were sold? _____

G. Which number occurs most often? _____

H. How many hot dogs were sold in all? _____

I. What is the average number of hot dogs sold? _____

# Are You Hungry?

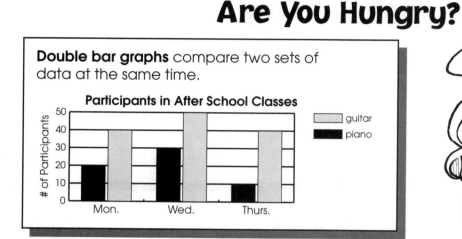

**Double bar graphs** compare two sets of data at the same time.

**Participants in After School Classes**

☐ guitar
■ piano

Complete the graph below.

Jon and Tia sold hot dogs and hamburgers for five weeks at the Saturday softball games.

hamburger sales for the five consecutive Saturdays: 10, 15, 5, 20, 30
hot dog sales for the five consecutive Saturdays: 20, 5, 25, 20, 15

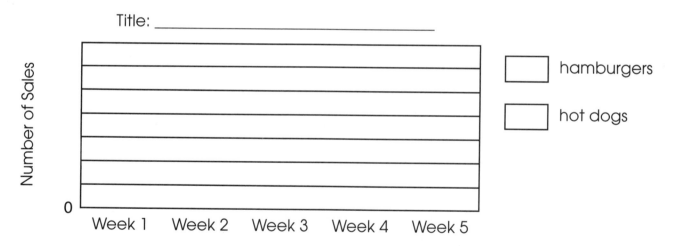

Title: _____

☐ hamburgers

☐ hot dogs

A. Which sold more the first week, hamburgers or hot dogs? _____

B. What was the total sale of hamburgers and hot dogs on week 3? _____

C. Which sold more during the five-week period, hamburgers or hot dogs? _____

D. What was the average number of hot dogs sold during the five-week period? _____

E. Which week came closest to that average? _____

F. Which had greater sales on the fifth week, hamburgers or hot dogs? _____

Name _____

# Average It Out

To calculate the **mean**:
1. Collect the data from the diagram.  4, 6, 6, 8, 6
2. Add and find the sum total.  4 + 6 + 6 + 8 + 6 = 30
3. Divide the sum total by the number of data entries (5).
   30 ÷ 5 = 6

The mean, 6, is the average.

**Children With Apples for Snacks**

Find the mean for each set of data.

A.

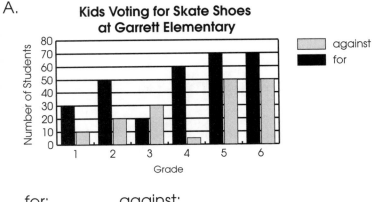

**Kids Voting for Skate Shoes
at Garrett Elementary**

for: _____    against: _____
   mean                           mean

B.

**Apples Brought for the Teacher**

red: _____    green: _____
   mean                           mean

C.

**Spring Food
Drive Donations**

| Stem | Leaf |
|------|------|
| 0 | 4 |
| 1 | 4, 5 |
| 2 | 1, 1 |
| 3 | 0, 0 |
| 4 | 1, 1, 2 |
| 5 | 0, 1 |

# of Pounds

_____ mean

D.

**Kids Wearing Bicycle Helmets**

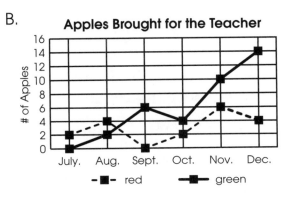

= 5 helmets

_____ mean

Name _____

# Dog Days

Mr. Yong Kim wanted to find out the average number of dogs that each student in his class owned.

the data collected: 3, 1, 2, 0, 1, 0, 2, 4, 1, 2, 3, 0, 0, 0, 1, 2, 2, 1, 1, 2, 3, 1, 2, 0, 1

data ordered from least to greatest: 0, 0, 0, 0, 0, 0, 1, 1, 1, 1, 1, 1, 1, 1, 1, 2, 2, 2, 2, 2, 2, 2, 3, 3, 3, 4

**Mode:** most frequent number: 1 (8 entries)

**Median:** middle number: 1 (12 numbers on the left and 12 on the right)

**Range:** Subtract the least number from the greatest number. (4 – 0 = 4)

**Mean:** the average (Find the total and divide by the number of entries.) 35 ÷ 25 = 1.4

Summary:   mode = 1
median = 1
range = 4
mean = 1.4

The students owned an average of 1.4 dogs each.

Analyze the following data. Find the range, median, mode, and mean.

A. the average number of seeds in the oranges on David's tree (20 samples taken)
Data: 3, 1, 2, 4, 5, 3, 1, 0, 1, 2, 1, 5, 6, 0, 3, 2, 1, 6, 6, 0

Order: _____

Range: _____    Median: _____    Mode: _____    Mean: _____

B. the average number of students with red hair at Lawson Elementary (20 classrooms sampled)

Data: 1, 3, 2, 0, 0, 1, 2, 5, 0, 1, 2, 1, 0, 2, 1, 0, 0, 0, 1, 0

Order: _____

Range: _____    Median: _____    Mode: _____    Mean: _____

C. students named "Katie" at Clearwater Elementary (25 classrooms sampled)
Data: 0, 1, 2, 0, 0, 1, 2, 1, 0, 0, 0, 1, 0, 0, 1, 0, 0, 0, 1, 0, 0, 0, 1, 0, 1

Order: _____

Range: _____    Median: _____    Mode: _____    Mean: _____

Name _____

# Cat's Face

Follow these steps to create a box plot for the data collected.

1.  Draw a line to chart all of the data.
    Data: 2, 4, 5, 5, 6, 7, 8, 12, 14, 16, 18, 21, 22, 25 (0 – 30)

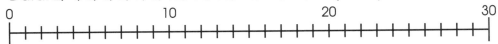

2.  Find the median of the data. Data: 2, 4, 5, 5, 6, 7, **8, 12**, 14, 16, 18, 21, 22, 25
    8 + 12 = 20   20 ÷ 2 = 10   The median equals 10.

3.  The length of the box is represented by a point showing the median of the lower half of the data and another point to show the median of the upper half of the data. The median of all the data is the point inside the box.

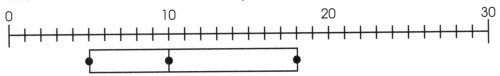

    Data: 2, 4, 5, **5**, 6, 7, 8,        12, 14, 16, **18**, 21, 22, 25

4.  The two line segments (whiskers) extending from each end of the box represent the range of the data.

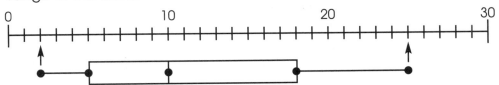

And there you have it—a box plot!

Use the data below to create a box plot.

Data: 3, 4, 7, 9, 11, 13, 17, 18, 22, 24, 27

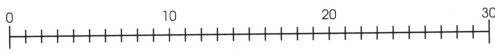

A.  What is the range of the data? _____

B.  What is the median of the entire data? _____

C.  What is the median of the lower half of the data? _____

D.  What is the median of the upper half of the data? _____

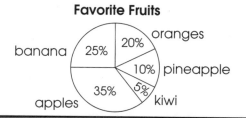

Name _____

# A Circle of Information

**Circle graphs** allow large amounts of information to be shown in a simple way.
Thirty students each cast one vote.
Ten percent voted for pineapple.
To find the exact number, figure 10% of 30.
    0.10 x 30 = 3
Three students voted for pineapple.

**Favorite Fruits**

banana 25% | 20% oranges | 10% pineapple | 5% kiwi | 35% apples

Answer each question using the graphs below.

**Poodle Colors**

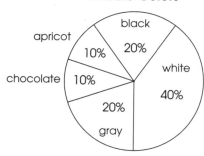

apricot 10% | black 20% | white 40% | gray 20% | chocolate 10%

Fifty poodle lovers were asked about their favorite color of poodle.

A. Which is the most popular color? _____

B. What percentage prefer black? _____
   Exactly how many is that? _____

C. How many poodle lovers prefer black over apricot?
   _____

Twenty-five students were asked how they liked to exercise.

D. Which exercise is the least popular?_____

E. Which exercise is the most popular?_____

F. How many prefer jogging over swimming? _____

**Favorite Exercise**

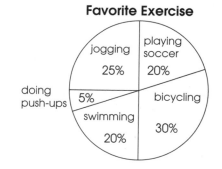

jogging 25% | playing soccer 20% | doing push-ups 5% | bicycling | swimming 20% | 30%

Place the correct percentages in each circle graph.

G. math—40%

   English—10%

   science—25%

   music—25%

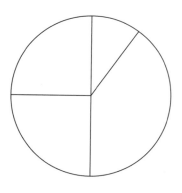

H. skateboarding—5%

   roller blading—35%

   scooters—10%

   bicycling—30%

   skate shoes—20%

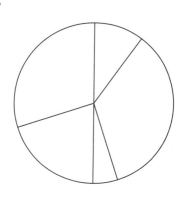

Math Practice: Grades 5–6

Name _____

# You Choose

Look at each collection of data. Then, choose the best graph type to organize that data collection. Enter the data and complete the graph. Label each graph with the appropriate title.

### Double Bar Graph

### Data Choices

| Favorite Music | |
|---|---|
| country | 30% |
| hip-hop | 10% |
| classical | 10% |
| gospel | 25% |
| rock 'n' roll | 25% |

### Circle Graph

**Fall City December Temperature Highs (degrees Fahrenheit)**

23°, 45°, 29°, 55°, 62°, 32°, 29°, 75°, 46°, 71°, 35°

| Stem | Leaf |
|---|---|
| 0 | |
| 1 | |
| 2 | |
| 3 | |
| 4 | |
| 5 | |
| 6 | |
| 7 | |
| 8 | |

### Stem-and-Leaf Plot

**Favorite Subject by Grade Level**

Fourth Grade
science: 50 votes
math: 70 votes

Fifth Grade
science: 30 votes
math: 65 votes

Sixth Grade
science: 50 votes
math: 60 votes

Name _____

# Predicting Events

When looking at data collected, predictions can be made. For example, if 50% of Ranchero Market's sales on Wednesday are advertised items, and it has been that way all year, we can predict that this coming Wednesday 50% of sales will be advertised items. Ranchero Market can prepare accordingly.

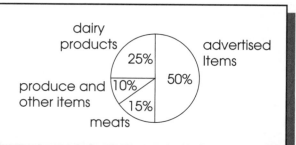

Use the graphs, diagrams, and data plots to make predictions.

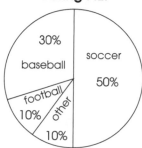

**Use of Free Time During P.E.**

A. Next time during free time, what choice of sports will 50% of the students probably make? _____

B. If students do not choose soccer, what choice are they most likely to make? _____

C. What percent of the students might choose something other than the three sports listed? _____

D. How likely is it that more students in fifth grade will sign up for band next year than sixth grade? _____

Why? _____

_____

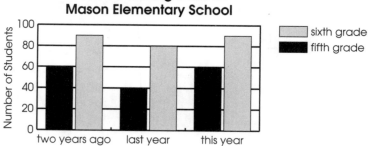

**Students Joining Band at Mason Elementary School**

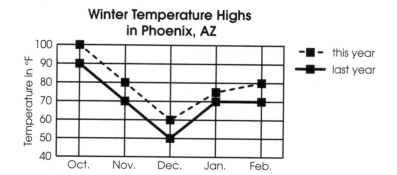

**Winter Temperature Highs in Phoenix, AZ**

E. Is it likely to snow in Phoenix in November based on the graph shown? _____

F. What temperature is it likely to be next year in February: 75°F or 120°F?

_____

Name _____

# Diagram the Data

**Venn diagrams** show how groups are related and hold common properties.

multiples of 2:  0, 2,  4,  6,  8,  10,  12
multiples of 3:  0, 3,  6,  9,  12,  15

The common multiples are inside the area where the circles intersect. Everything outside this area is related only to the labeled circle.

**Multiples of 2 and 3**

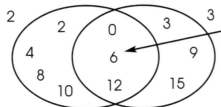

common properties (everything inside where the two circles intersect)

Complete each Venn diagram using the data given.

A.  Jonathan compared birth dates in his classroom for the months of March and April.

March: 3, 8, 14, 22, 24, 30

April: 4, 8, 17, 22, 24, 28

**Birth Dates for March and April**

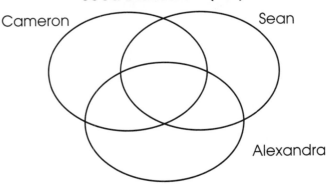

B.  Mark, Heather, and Gwen compared the multiples of 4 and 5.

multiples of 4: 0, 4, 8, 12, 16, 20

multiples of 5: 0, 5, 10, 15, 20, 25

**Multiples of 4 and 5**

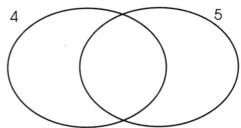

C.  Cameron, Sean, and Alexandra compared diameters for the seeds they each found.

Cameron: 0.5 cm, 1 cm, 1.5 cm, 2 cm

Sean: 0.5 cm, 3.5 cm, 4.5 cm, 5 cm

Alexandra: 0.25 cm, 0.5 cm, 2.5 cm, 3 cm

**Seed Diameters (cm)**

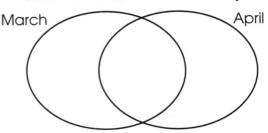

Name _____

# What Are the Possibilities?

What is the probability that you will pick a blue marble out of the box?

First, count how many blue marbles there are in the box. (2)

Second, count the total number of marbles in the box. (4)

$\frac{2}{4} = \frac{1}{2}$

The ratio is 2:4. The probability is 2 out of 4.

This reduces to 1/2. The probability is 1/2.

A. Find the probability of the spinner landing on

red. _____        green. _____

blue. _____       yellow. _____

B. Find the probability of picking out of the "possibility" box the letter

s. _____        x. _____

b. _____        i. _____

p. _____        y. _____

C. Find the probability of the spinner landing on

an even number. _____        the number 3. _____

a number 5 or greater. _____        a number divisible by 2. _____

an odd number. _____        a multiple of 2. _____

a number less than 5. _____

D. Find the probability of picking out of the box a

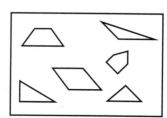

triangle. _____        rectangular prism. _____

polygon. _____        right triangle. _____

rhombus. _____        quadrilateral. _____

Name _____

# Is It Equally Likely?

Words can be used to describe the probability of an event taking place.
**Likely:** there is a good probability that it will happen.
**Unlikely:** there is a good probability that it will not happen.
**Certain:** it will happen for sure.
**Equally likely:** there is an equal chance that it will or will not happen.
**Impossible:** it will not happen.

Use the terms **likely** and **unlikely** to describe the probability of an event taking place.

A. It will rain today.

_____

B. Everyone left for the game.
The pizza will be eaten now.

_____

C. Chompers will bark.

_____

D. You will find a triangle in the box.

_____

Use the terms **certain, equally likely,** and **impossible** to describe whether an event will or will not take place.

E. Pick a marble or cube out of the box. Your pick will be a:

cube: _____

marble: _____

cube or a marble: _____

pencil: _____

Name _____

# Forks in the Road

A **tree diagram** shows how many choices there are.

Earl goes to the pet store.
There is a choice of two colors of poodles: apricot or white.

There is a choice of three sizes of each color: tea cup, toy, or standard.

There is a choice of male or female.

How many choices does Earl have to pick from in all? Twelve choices in all.

Draw a tree diagram for each set of information. Tell how many choices there are in all.

A. Deborah goes to the grocery store to buy some fruit.
   1. She wants either: apples or grapes.
   2. There are two different colors for each: red or green.

   There are _____ choices.

B. Bill wants to buy a kite.
   1. There are two types: box or regular.
   2. There are three types of material: silk, plastic, or paper.
   3. There are three colors to choose from: blue, white, or red.

   There are _____ choices.

C. Mark wants to design a T-shirt.
   1. T-shirt backgrounds are white or blue.
   2. Ink colors are black or yellow.
   3. Sizes are small, medium, or large.

   There are _____ choices.

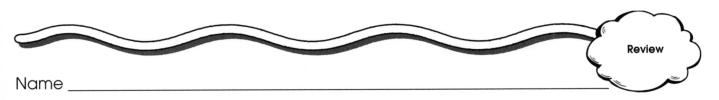

Name _____

# Time to Review

A. What does the dashed line represent?

_____

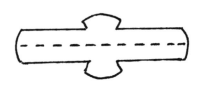

B. Identify this polygon.

_____

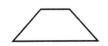

C. What is the ordered pair for the location on the grid? _____

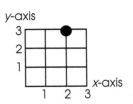

D. What is the term for a pair of lines that never intersect? _____

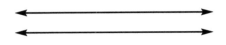

E. What is the name for this solid figure?

_____

F. Each face of a pyramid is a

_____.

G. Two rays come together at a vertex to form an

_____.

H. What is the term for this movement?

_____

I. How do these polygons compare to each other? _____

Name _____

J. What is the shortest path from point A to point B? _____

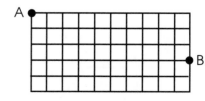

(Each length of width of  = 1 mile.)

K. Match the front view.

a. b. c.

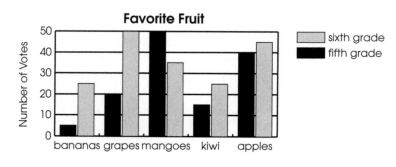

Use the graphs to answer the questions.

**Favorite Fruit**

Number of Votes

50
40
30
20
10
0

bananas grapes mangoes kiwi apples

sixth grade
fifth grade

L. Which fruit was the most popular in sixth grade? _____

M. Which fruit was the least popular in fifth grade? _____

N. What was the total number of votes in fifth grade? _____

O. What was the difference in the number of skaters in May? _____

P. Which month had the highest attendance of skaters? _____

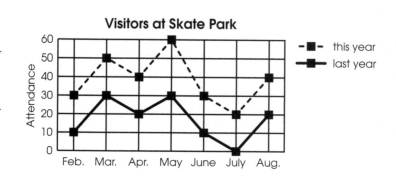

**Visitors at Skate Park**

Attendance

60
50
40
30
20
10
0

Feb. Mar. Apr. May June July Aug.

this year
last year

Name _____

Use the table to answer the questions.

**Animal Shows**

| dogs | 8:00 A.M. |
|------|-----------|
| cats | 9:00 A.M. |
| ferrets | 10:00 A.M. |
| turtles | 12:00 P.M. |
| rabbits | 2:00 P.M. |

Q. How many hours after the dog show does the ferret show start? _____

R. How many hours before the rabbit show does the dog show start?

_____

S. What is the average or mean of this data?    2, 4, 6, 1, 2

_____

T. What is the probability of pulling a red marble out of the box?

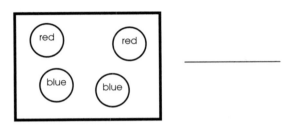

_____

U. You are given a choice of a blue or red shirt with white or yellow print. The shirt comes in sizes small, medium, or large. Draw a tree diagram to represent your choices.

How many choices are there in all?

Name _____

V. Figure the area of the rectangle.

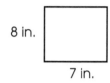

8 in.

7 in.

A = _____

W. What is the area of the triangle?

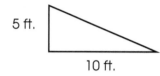

5 ft.

10 ft.

A = _____

X. What is the circumference of this circle? Formula: $C = \pi \times d$

6 in.

C = _____

Y. Write an addition problem using fractions. Shade in the boxes to show the problem.

_____ + _____ = _____

Z. Write the fact family for the numbers 3, 4, and 7.

_____

_____

_____

_____

**Page 4**
A. three thousand, one hundred eighty-seven; B. twenty-one thousand, sixty-seven; C. four hundred twenty-seven; D. one million, eight hundred thousand, two hundred thirty-four; E. 400 + 50 + 6; F. 40,000 + 3,000 + 500 + 60 + 7; G. 200,000 + 30,000 + 4,000 + 600 + 70 + 8; H. 8,443; I. 40 1/6; J. -6

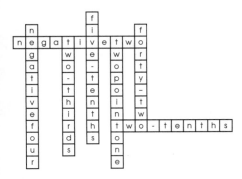

**Page 5**
A. four thousand; B. one million; C. sixty thousand; D. seventy million; E. five hundred million; F. nine billion; G.–M.

**Page 6**
A. 194 students; B. Flipperflop, 580,000 people; C. 2,348 students; D. milk, 23,041 pints; E. 2,374 pairs of skate shoes; F. 38,603 hot dogs and pretzels

**Page 7**
A. 2,345; 3,245; 4,324; 5,432; B. 43; 4,237; 42,006; 456,123; C. 3; 2,404; 45,007; 435,132; D. 1/6; 1/3; E. 2/10; 3/5; F. 1/4; 1/3; G. -10; -9; -7; -4; H. 3.2; 3.6; 6.4; 6.9; I. 0.0002; 0.002; 0.02; 0.2; 33.332; 3.2; 3.0032; 0.332; 0.032

**Page 8**
A. 7.5, 10, 0.3; B. 242, 3.5, 19; C. 4, 9, 50; D. 6.3, 12, 12.5; E. $85.00, $34.00, $51.00; F. $12.50, $7.50, $5.00; G. $39.00, $11.70, $27.30; H. $20.95, $10.48, $10.48

**Page 9**
A. $3^4$; B. $6^3$; C. $9^8$; D. 8; 36; 256; 343; E. 9; 1; 81; 81; F. 64; 32; 0; 27; G. 300; 8,000; 6,000,000; H. 60,000; 400,000; 500; I. $7 \times 10^3$; $5 \times 10^3$; $6 \times 10^5$; J. $8 \times 10^6$; $4 \times 10^4$; $3 \times 10^9$

**Page 10**
A. 2 x 2 x 7, 3 x 7, 2 x 2 x 2 x 2, 2 x 2 x 2 x 2 x 3; B. 2 x 2 x 3 x 3, 2 x 2 x 2 x 5, 2 x 2 x 2 x 2 x 2, 2 x 2 x 2 x 3; C. 3 x 5, 2 x 3 x 3, 2 x 2 x 5, 2 x 5 x 5; D. 3 x 3 x 3, 2 x 3 x 5, 5 x 11, 2 x 3 x 7

**Page 11**
A. 4/12 = 1/3; B. 7/20; C. 3/8; D. 1/6; E. 2/9; F. 3/15 = 1/5; G.–L. Check students' shadings.; M. 6/8 = 3/4; N. 5/6; O. 7/10; P. 5/12

**Page 12**
A. 0.5, 0.4, 0.1, 0.1; B. 0.2, 0.25, 0.05, 0.75; C. 0.5, 0.5, 0.5, numerator = 1/2 denominator, decimal = 0.5; D. 0.2, 0.4, 0.6, as value increases 1/5, decimal increases by 0.2; E. 0.25, 0.5, 0.75, as value increases 1/4, decimal increases by 0.25; F. 0.5, 0.8, 0.6̄6, no pattern; 0.125, 0.375, 0.625, 0.875, as fraction increases by 2/8 = 1/4, decimal increases by 0.25

**Page 13**
A. 60%, 10%, 75%, 90%; B. 25%, 6%, 28%, 15%; C. 80%, 50%, 35%, 40%

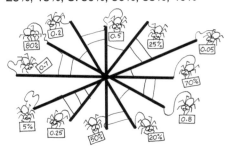

**Page 14**
A. 0.25, 25%; B. 0.75, 75%; C. 0.1, 10%; D. 0.5, 50%; E. 0.2, 20%; F. 0.125, 12.5%; G. 0.05, 5%; H. 0.8, 80%

**Page 15**
A. 6, 18, 9, 8, 30; B. 20, 4, 8, 24, 72; C. 15, 6, 6, 12, 10; D. 10, 42, 10, 14, 12; E. 21, 36, 14, 30, 15; F. 24, 45, 40, 12, 12

**Page 16**
A. 3, 7, 5; B. 4, 9, 10; C. 6, 7, 5; D. 4, 8, 3; E. 6, 9; F. 5, 12; G. 4, 8; H. 3, 10; I. 4, 6; J. 7, 8

**Page 17**
1/2 = acute; 2/3 = sphere; 1/4 = cube; 2/5 = obtuse; 1/8 = ray; 1/6 = rhombus

**Page 18**
A. 4, 24, 12, 1, 4; B. 15, 7, 5, 4, 3; C. 4, 8, 4, 1, 4; D. 4, 9, 3; E. 2, 33, 6; F. 3, 32, 35; G. 1/2 = 8/16; H. 2/4 = 8/16; I. 3/5 = 9/15

**Page 19**
A. 1/4 < 1/2, 2/4 = 4/8, 1/9 < 1/3; B. 1/10 < 1/5, 1/3 > 1/6, 1/12 < 3/12; C. <, >, >, <; D. >, >, <, <; E. <, >, =, >

**Page 20**
A. 24, 8, 15, 6, 55; B. 14, 18, 22.5, 24, 6; C. 16, 11, 9, 16, 24; D. 36, 36, 28; E. 8.125, 18.75, 96; 48

**Page 21**
A. 1/2, 1/2, 1/2, 5/16; B. 1/2, 5/12, 1, 2/3; C. 13/21, 5/8, 11/30, 7/12; D. 5/18, 7/12, 5/6, 7/16

**Page 22**
A. 5/8, 1/8, 1/4, 7/18; B. 1/2, 1/6, 3/8, 0; C. 2/5, 1/6, 1/20, 4/21; D. 7/15, 7/20, 17/56, 7/18

**Page 23**
A. 1/6, 1/9; B. 2/10, 1/10; C. 1/4, 1/32; D. 2/14, 4/42 = 2/21; E. 1/12, 1/15, 1/18, 2/15, 1/6; F. 1/30, 2/5, 1/12, 2/35, 3/20; G. 1/24, 3/28, 3/35, 1/6, 1/9; H. 3/14, 1/6, 1/12, 1/6, 1/9

**Page 24**
A. 11 3/10, 8 3/4, 13 5/8, 10 7/12, 20 1/2; B. 14 3/4, 11 5/6, 14 4/5, 2 1/2, 7 2/5; C. 7 8/15, 3 1/3, 6 7/16, 6 1/4, 3 5/8

**Page 25**
A. 45, 72, 50, 120; B. 24, 1 4/5, 4/21, 2/3; C. 2/3, 1 1/2; D. 1 1/2, 3 3/5; E. 3/8, 2 2/3

**Page 26**
A. 10 1/2, 6, 16 2/3, 8 2/3; B. 4 2/3, 3, 3 1/8, 1/2; C. 2/5, 1/2, 5/6, 13/16; D. 6 1/2, 4 4/5, 7 3/5, 5; E. 1 7/8, 3 3/10, 1 7/8, 14

**Page 27**
A. 486; 1,520; 1,734; 2,051; 4,754; B. 8,491; 10,034; 7,600; 10,799; 8,859; C. 7,345; 4,103; 8,008; 322,469; 389,184; D. 1,077; 4,986; 11,083; 11,072; 12,676

**Page 28**
A. 158; 307; 258; B. 253; 2,971; 5,407; C. 3,914; 2,385; 4,819; 6,834; 6,720; D. 4,028; 2,382; 2,425; 6,102; 6,317; E. 23,242; 27,395; 294,847; 124,826; 296,758

**Page 29**
A. $6.44, $16.54, $5.09, $2.97, $6.33; B. $10.79, $5.63, $76.39, $2.09, $85.75; C. $363.31, $80.68, $375.27, $190.31, $949.81; D. $618.03, $925.56, $331.11, $176.66, $153.86; $7.19

## Page 30
A. 0.67, 1.128, 12.01; B. 6.921, 8.465;
C. 38.658, 859.18, 41.855; D. 4.3162,
29.84, 3.3061, 38.3652

## Page 31
A. 1.66, 1.09, 57.02; B. 0.035, 1.011,
3.903; C. 1.884, 32.2119, 3.137, 3.4832,
0.3468; D. 54.1786, 8.122, 8.854, 78.34,
3.666

## Page 32
A. 3 x 2; B. 5 x 3; C. 2 x 6; D. 4 x 7;
E.–P. Check students' arrays.

## Page 33
A. 4 x 3 = 12; B. 2 x 5 = 10; C. 3 x 6 = 18;
D. 4 x 4 = 16; E. 3 x 10 = 30; F. 2 x 7 =
14; G. 3 x 8 = 24; H. 3 x 9 = 27;
I.–P. Check students' drawings.

## Page 34

## Page 35
A. 192; 259; 245; 224; B. 186; 240; 5,792;
2,528; C. 2,667; 1,060; 2,988; 1,620;
D. 24,416; 28,854; 29,463; 40,860

## Page 36
A. 868; 1,029; 1,426; B. 1,280; 7,452;
3,552; C. 10,672; 22,134; 57,316; 68,376;
57,892; D. 104,244; 71,478; 212,432;
191,226; 527,552

## Page 37
A. 72,534; 72,072; 52,875; 52,650;
63,240; B. 32,736; 43,648; 90,496;
83,316; 119,709; C. 961,704; 1,754,298;
369,376; 324,386; 445,056

## Page 38
A. 24.368, 1.33, 2.808, 6.060, 0.248,
0.246; B. 41.208, 50.760, 71.0151,
16.896, 67.648, 831.09

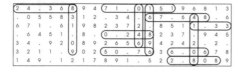

## Page 39
A. 8 R2, 9 R3, 8 R4, 9 R4, 5 R3; B. 45
R2, 35 R2, 46 R6, 37 R3, 89 R5; C. 412
R3, 879, 798 R2, 247 R1, 465 R4

## Page 40
A. 9 R4, 8 R12, 5 R20, 6, 8 R4; B. 9, 18,
26 R25, 21 R44, 63; C. 314 R13, 114,
127, 346 R3, 125 R52

## Page 41
A. 9, 7, 21 R75, 36 R45; B. 23 R40, 113,
46 R4, 315 R12; C. 127 R150, 104, 226
R50, 149 R147

## Page 42
A. 20 R7, 50 R4, 90 R3, 80 R1, 70 R8;
B. 120 R6, 206 R3, 130 R5, 207 R1, 420
R4; C. 102 R34, 120, 450 R18, 130 R63,
280 R4

## Page 43
A. 1.8, 2.6, 3.7, 4.6, 89; B. 23.6, 45.9,
78.5, 69.1, 38.6; C. 6.3, 2.78, 36.8

## Page 44
A. 10°, 10 P.M.; B. $6.00; C. 21; D. 2,
$520; E. 1; F. 6

## Page 45
A. He also has a pet frog., $1.25; B. He is
also cooking 5 rolls in the microwave., 3
pints; C. Silver is her favorite color of
pencils., 5 pencils; D. Most are small, but
some are large., 3 fish; E. It takes her 10
minutes to walk from home to her friend
Gwen's house., 3:05 P.M.; F. His favorite
sport is softball. He spends 3 hours a
week practicing., $15; G. Their dads go
fishing for two hours each time they are
at the pond., 105 tadpoles

## Page 46
A. addition, $9.92; B. division, 82 lb.;
C. addition, 7/12; D. multiplication, 42;
E. subtraction, $13.11; F. multiplication,
$1,287.30

## Page 47
A. 8 + 12 = 20, 12 + 8 = 20, 20 − 12 = 8,
20 − 8 = 12; B. 25 + 32 = 57, 32 + 25 =
57, 57 − 32 = 25, 57 − 25 = 32; C. 3/9 +
4/9 = 7/9, 4/9 + 3/9 = 7/9, 7/9 − 4/9 = 3/9,
7/9 − 3/9 = 4/9; D. 0.8 + 0.4 = 1.2, 0.4 +
0.8 = 1.2, 1.2 − 0.4 = 0.8, 1.2 − 0.8 = 0.4;
E. 3.2 + 4.8 = 8, 4.8 + 3.2 = 8, 8 − 4.8 =
3.2, 8 − 3.2 = 4.8; F. 3/11 + 6/11 = 9/11,
6/11 + 3/11 = 9/11, 9/11 − 6/11 = 3/11,
9/11 − 3/11 = 6/11; G. 7 x 8 = 56, 8 x 7 =
56, 56 ÷ 8 = 7, 56 ÷ 7 = 8; H. 0.8 x 0.5 =
0.40, 0.5 x 0.8 = 0.40, 0.40 ÷ 0.5 = 0.8,
0.40 ÷ 0.8 = 0.5; I. 1/3 x 1/2 = 1/6, 1/2 x
1/3 = 1/6, 1/6 ÷ 1/2 = 1/3, 1/6 ÷ 1/3 = 1/2

## Page 48
A. 621; 400 + 200 = 600; B. 105; 80 + 30
= 110; C. 9,240; 7,000 + 2,000 = 9,000;
D. 233; 700 − 500 = 200; E. 9; 50 − 40 =
10; F. 1,508; 3,000 − 2,000 = 1,000;
G. 10.4; 6 + 4 = 10; H. 174.60; 30 x 5 =
150; I. 49.23; 30 + 20 = 50; J. 4,120; 800
x 5 = 4,000; K. 1,656; 70 x 20 = 1,400;
L. 73,278; 8,000 x 9 = 72,000; M. 32; 200
÷ 6 = 33 R2; N. 278; 1,000 ÷ 5 = 200;
O. 298; 9,000 ÷ 30 = 300

## Page 49
A. $5, $5.18; 800, 816; 5,000, 5,063;
B. 6,000, 6,058; 4,000, 4,137; 400, 427;
C. $14, $13.79; $7, $7.06; $13, $12.62;
D. 1,000, 983; $11, $10.99; 9,000, 9,090

## Page 50

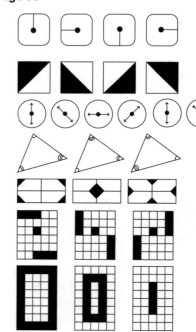

## Page 51

| A | B | C | D | E | F |
|---|---|---|---|---|---|
| 2 | 3 | 4 | 5 | 6 | 7 |
| 3 | 5 | 7 | 9 | 11 | 13 |
| 3 | 6 | 10 | 15 | 21 | 28 |

| 3 | 4 | 5 | 6 | 7 |
|---|---|---|---|---|

4, 12, 20, 28; 8

**Page 115**

A. **Birth Dates for March and April**

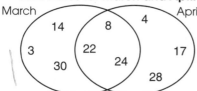

March        April
14      8      4
3    22    17
30    24
28

B. **Multiples of 4 and 5**

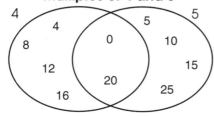

4                        5
4        5      5
8      0      10
12          15
16    20    25

C. **Seed Diameters (cm)**

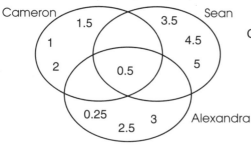

Cameron              Sean
1    1.5    3.5
2          4.5
0.5    5
0.25    3
2.5    Alexandra

**Page 116**

A. red: 1/2, green: 1/8, blue: 1/4, yellow: 1/8; B. s: 2/11, b: 1/11, p: 1/11, x: 0, i: 3/11, y: 1/11; C. even: 3/8, ≥ 5: 1/2, odd: 5/8, < 5: 1/2, 3: 1/4, ÷ 2: 3/8, M2: 3/8; D. triangle: 1/2, rectangular prism: 0, polygon: 1, right triangle: 1/3, rhombus: 1/6, quadrilateral: 1/3

**Page 117**

A. likely; B. unlikely; C. likely; D. unlikely; E. cube: equally likely, marble: equally likely, cube or marble: certain, pencil: impossible

**Page 118**

A. 4 choices

apples — red, green
grapes — red, green

B. 18 choices

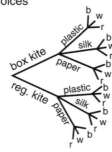

box kite — plastic, silk, paper (b, w, r)
reg. kite — plastic, silk, paper (b, w, r)

C. 12 choices

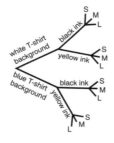

white T-shirt background — black ink, yellow ink (S, M, L)
blue T-shirt background — black ink, yellow ink (S, M, L)

**Page 119**

A. line of symmetry; B. trapezoid; C. (2, 3); D. parallel; E. rectangular prism or cube; F. triangle; G. angle; H. flip; I. similar

**Page 120**

J. 13 miles; K. b; L. grapes; M. bananas; N. 130; O. 30; P. May

**Page 121**

Q. 2; R. 6; S. 3; T. 1/2; U. 12 choices

blue shirt — white print, yellow print (S, M, L)
red shirt — white print, yellow print (S, M, L)

**Page 122**

V. 56 in.²; W. 25 ft.²; X. 18.84 in.; Y. Answers will vary.; Z. 3 + 4 = 7, 4 + 3 = 7, 7 − 3 = 4, 7 − 4 = 3

**Page 97**
A. 37° C, BT; B. 0° C, FP; C. 100° C, BP; D. 78° C; E. 20° C, RT; F. 40° C, -20° C, 70° C; G. 125° C, 37° C, 104° C; H. T-shirt; I. jacket; J. cold drink; K. hot drink

**Page 98**
A. April 28; B. April 9; C. April 26; D. April 10; E. April 5; F. yes; G. Tuesday; H. 4 days; I. 2 weeks; J. yes; K. January 26

**Page 99**
A. 4 hr. 17 min.; B. 8:25 A.M.; C. 7 d. 8 hr.; D. 1. 10:00 A.M.; 2. 12:22 P.M.; E. 1. 2:25 P.M.; 2. 3:00 P.M.

**Page 100**
A. 11 hr. 39 min., 19 hr. 16 min., 54 min. 47 sec.; B. 6 d. 11 hr., 16 hr. 1 min., 10 wk. 2 d.; C. 18 d 12 hr., 20 hr. 34 min., 18 wk.; D. 2 hr. 54 min., 6 hr. 49 min., 14 min., 59 sec.; E. 1 d. 21 hr., 3 wk. 5 d., 11 hr. 40 min.; F. 33 min. 47 sec., 9 min. 11 sec.; 4 hr. 52 min.

**Page 101**
A. no; B. yes; C. the higher the ranking of love of reading, the more books one bought; D. the greater the ranking of love of mathematics, the more hours spent on math projects; E.–F. Answers will vary.

**Page 102**
A. 7 P.M., 4 P.M., 6 P.M.; B. 6 P.M., 9 P.M., 7 P.M.; C. 11 A.M., 10 A.M., 9 A.M.; D. 2 P.M.; E. Subtract 3 hours., 4:25 A.M.; F. Add 1 hour., 12:10 P.M.; G. Add 2 hours., 5:28 P.M.; H. Subtract 3 hours., 1:00 P.M.

**Page 103**
A. 2 drawings; B. 4 more drawings; C. 30 drawings; D. Gwen; E. increase; F. 2 more hours; G. Sept. 15; H. increase; I. Zoe; J. up

**Page 104**
A. 185 boxes; B. fresh fruit; C. 1,900 pounds; D. 1,567 cans of tuna; E. 155 boxes of spaghetti; F. year 4; G. fish; H. 21,000; I. 6,360; J. 11,820 more

**Page 105**
A. 50; B. 10–11 A.M.; C. 54; D. 8–9 A.M., 12–1 P.M., 9–10 A.M., 11 A.M.–12 P.M., 10–11 A.M.; E. 75; F. 20; G. lasagna and bean burritos; H. 425; I. 1–2 P.M.; J. 646; K. 154

**Page 106**
A. week 4; B. 24 pairs; C. 76 pairs; D. 4, 8, 16, 20, 28; E. Golden Delicious; F. 36; G. 3; H. 72

**Page 107**
A. 18; B. 13; C. 46; D. twice; E. 12; F. 37; G. 22; H. 262; I. 21 5/6

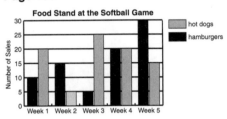

Attendance at Skating Park

| Stem | Leaf |
|------|------|
| 0 | |
| 1 | 3, 3, 8, 8, 8 |
| 2 | 0, 3, 7 |
| 3 | 1, 1, 5, 8 |
| 4 | 0, 2, 6, 6 |

Hot Dog Sales

| Stem | Leaf |
|------|------|
| 0 | |
| 1 | 2, 2, 3, 7 |
| 2 | 1, 2, 2, 2, 2 |
| 3 | 0, 2, 7 |

**Page 108**

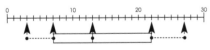

A. hot dogs; B. 30; C. hot dogs; D. 17; E. week 5; F. hamburgers

**Page 109**
A. 50, 27.5; B. 3, 6; C. 30, D. 21

**Page 110**
A. 0, 0, 0, 1, 1, 1, 1, 2, 2, 2, 3, 3, 3, 4, 5, 5, 6, 6, 6; 6, 2, 1, 2.6; B. 0, 0, 0, 0, 0, 0, 0, 0, 1, 1, 1, 1, 1, 2, 2, 2, 2, 3, 5; 5, 1, 0, 1.1; C. 0, 0, 0, 0, 0, 0, 0, 0, 0, 0, 0, 0, 0, 0, 0, 0, 1, 1, 1, 1, 1, 1, 1, 1, 2, 2; 2, 0, 0, 0.48

**Page 111**
A. 24; B. 13; C. 7; D. 22

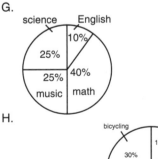

**Page 112**
A. white; B. 20%, 10 poodle lovers; C. 5 poodle lovers; D. doing push-ups; E. bicycling; F. 1.25

G.

science  English
10%
25%
25%   40%
music  math

H.

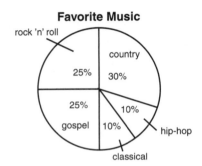

bicycling  scooters
10%
30%          35%  roller blading
20%
5%
skate shoes  skateboarding

**Page 113**

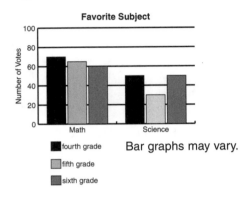

Favorite Subject
Number of Votes
Math   Science
■ fourth grade    Bar graphs may vary.
▢ fifth grade
▨ sixth grade

**Favorite Music**

rock 'n' roll
country
25%    30%
25%    10%
gospel  10%  hip-hop
classical

Fall City December Temperature Highs (degrees Fahrenheit)

| Stem | Leaf |
|------|------|
| 0 | |
| 1 | |
| 2 | 3, 9, 9 |
| 3 | 2, 5 |
| 4 | 5, 6 |
| 5 | 5 |
| 6 | 2 |
| 7 | 1, 5 |
| 8 | |

**Page 114**
A. soccer; B. baseball; C. 10%; D. not very likely; E. no; F. 75° F

**Page 72**

A.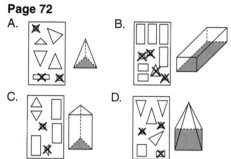

B.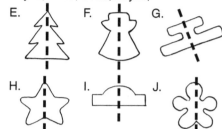

C.

D.

**Page 73**

Check students' angles.

**Page 74**

A. 20°, 80°, 50°, 10°; B. 110°, 30°, 60°, 140°; C. 130°, obtuse; 30°, right; 90°, right; 50°, acute; D. 120°, obtuse; 70°, acute; 140°, obtuse; 60°, acute

**Page 75**

A. slide or flip, flip, slide or flip, flip; B. slide, slide, turn, flip; C. slide or flip, flip, turn, turn; D. turn, slide, flip, flip; E. slide, flip, turn, flip

**Page 76**

Lines may vary.

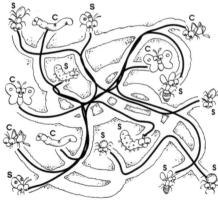

**Page 77**

A. 3.5 miles; B. 5.5 miles; C. 5 miles; D. 21 miles; E. 17 miles

**Page 78**

Paths may vary. Possible paths include:

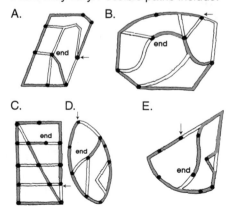

**Page 79**

A. yes; B. no; C. no; D. yes;

E. F. G.

H. I. J.

K. yes; L. no; M. yes; N. no

**Page 80**

Top View: B, A, D, C; Side View: D, B, A, C; Check students' figures.

**Page 81**

A. 16 in.; B. 16 m; C. 46 yd.; D. 90 cm; E. 33.1 m; F. 41 cm; G. 70 mi.; H. 31.6 mm; I. yd.; J. mi.; K. ft.; L. in.; M. m; N. km; O. cm; P. cm; Q. mm

**Page 82**

A. 40 m²; B. 36 in.²; C. 4 ft.²; D. 77 in.²; E. 32 cm²; F. 42 ft.²; G. 25 mm²; H. 120 mi.²; I. 36 cm²; J. 29.16 m²; K. 25.2 in.²; L. 32 ft.²; 199 ft.²

**Page 83**

A. 24 cm²; B. 8 ft.²; C. 22 m²; D. 26.25 in.²; E. 5.76 mm²; F. 2.625 ft.²; G. 32 in.²; H. 34 cm²; I. 94 m²; J. 87 cm²; K. 128 in.²; L. 184 mm²; M. 224 in.²; N. 344 mm²

**Page 84**

A. 16.4 cm²; B. 75 in.²; C. 5.4 m²; D. 96 cm²; E. 22.4 ft.²; F. 32.2 ft.²; G. 87.36 mm²; H. 48 cm²; I. 110 m²; J. 156 cm²

**Page 85**

A. $A = s^2$, area, 16 ft.²; B. $A = l$ x $w$, area, 24 ft.²; C. $P$ = add all sides, perimeter, 8 ft.; D. $P$ = add all sides, perimeter, 450 m; E. $A = 1/2(b$ x $h)$, area, 150 ft.²; F. $A = 1/2(b$ x $h)$, area, 165 cm²; G. $A = l$ x $w$, area, 12 m², 12 plots

**Page 86**

A. 72 ft.²; B. 108 cm²; C. 94 ft.²; D. 360 in.²; E. 616 yd.²; F. 468 in.²; G. 328 m²; H. 352 cm²

**Page 87**

A. 60 m³; B. 160 in.³; C. 41.354 m³; D. 240 mm³; E. 38.4 in.³; F. 384 cm³; G. 44 ft.³; H. 66.3 in.³; yes, V = 270 ft.³

**Page 88**

A. 9.42 ft.; B. 6.28 ft.; C. 6.28 ft.; D. 6.28 ft.; E. 12.56 ft.; F. 9.42 ft.; G. 12.56 ft., total = 62.8 ft.; H. 3.14 ft.; I. 6.28 ft.; J. 9.42 ft.; total = 18.84 ft.; K. 9.42 in.; L. 15.7 in.; total = 25.12 in.; M. 94.2 cm; N. 94.2 cm; total = 188.4 cm

**Page 89**

A. 314 m²; B. 113.04 yd.²; C. 254.34 m²; D. 200.96 mm²; E. 28.26 cm²; F. 3.14 m²; G. 12.56 m²; H. 78.5 yd.²; I. 50.24 in.²; J. 153.86 cm²; 11.44 m²

**Page 90**

A. 75.36 + 12.56 + 12.56 = 100.48 mm²; B. 251.2 + 50.24 + 50.24 = 351.68 cm²; C. 25.12 + 3.14 + 3.14 = 31.4 in.²; D. 62.8 + 12.56 + 12.56 = 87.92 mm²; E. 150.72 + 28.26 + 28.26 = 207.24 ft.²; F. 131.88 + 28.26 + 28.26 = 188.4 cm²; G. 100.48 + 50.24 + 50.24 = 200.96 in.²; H. 301.44 + 50.24 + 50.24 = 401.92 m²; I. 125.6 + 12.56 + 12.56 = 150.72 in.²

**Page 91**

A. 2, 48; B. 1/2, 1/4; C. 2,000, 2; D. 5, 96; E. 1, 6, 3, 1; F. 1, 2, 2, 1; G. 1/4, 1/2, 1/16, 1/8; H. gallons; I. pints; J. cups; K. gallons; L. quarts; M. gallons; N. cups

**Page 92**

A. 1, 1 1/2, 24; B. 4, 2, 21; C. 36, 3, 9; D. 1/2, 30, 132; E. 7 yd. 1 ft.; F. 20 ft. 3 in.; G. 22 yd. 2 ft.; H. 8 in.; I. miles; J. feet; K. feet; L. inches; M. yards; N. 4 inches; O. 1 1/2 inches; P. 3 inches

**Page 93**

A. 2, 30, 3; B. 50, 70, 9; C. 3, 20, 1; D. mm; E. cm; F. m; G. km; H. cm; Their eyes never become dry.

**Page 94**

A. 1; 1; 4,000; B. 5,000; 3; 9,000; C. 8,000; 2; 4,000; D. L; E. kL; F. g; G. kg; H. mg; Chirping is for the birds and crickets, too!

**Page 95**

A. <, >, >, =; B. >, =, <, <; C. <, <, >, <; D. >, >, <, <; E. 1 m; F. 8 ft.; G. 1 mi.; H. 1 km; I. 1 m; J. 4 ft.; K. 1 L; L. 3 gal.; M. 5 L; N. 3 lb.; O. 1 kg; P. 1 lb.; Q. 2 m of rope; R. 8 L of olive oil; S. 1 mi. of yarn; T. 5 kg of potatoes

**Page 96**

A. 98.6° F, BT; B. 200° F; C. 32° F, FP; D. 68° F, RT; E. 212° F, BP; F. Water in pan boils., 212° F; G. Water in glass freezes., 32° F; H. Snowman will melt., 44° F

**Page 52**
A. 10, 5, 0; B. 2, 2.5, 3; C. 5/15, 6/18, 7/21; D. 25, 36, 49; E. x 2, 12, 14, 16, 18; F. ÷ 3, 4, 5, 6, 7; G. ÷ 4, 1.00, 1.25, 1.50, 1.75; H. + 5, 9, 10, 11; I. + 0.5, 0.9, 1.0, 1.1, 1.2

J. K. L.

**Page 53**
A. commutative property; B. distributive property; C. associative property; D. associative property; E. commutative property; F. distributive property; G. commutative property; H. 5 + 7 = 12, 7 + 5 = 12, commutative property

**Page 54**
A. 6 + 2 = 8, 2 + 6 = 8; B. 4 + 12 = 16, 12 + 4 = 16; C. 3/10 + 2/5 = 7/10, 2/5 + 3/10 = 7/10; D. 2/9 + 1/3 = 5/9, 1/3 + 2/9 = 5/9; E. 5 x 2 = 10, 2 x 5 = 10; F. 5 x 6 = 30, 6 x 5 = 30

**Page 55**
A. 6 + (4 + 6) = 16, (6 + 4) + 6 = 16; B. 8 + (6 + 3) = 17, (8 + 6) + 3 = 17; C. 1/5 + (1/3 + 3/15) = 11/15, (1/5 + 1/3) + 3/15 = 11/15; D. 1/2 + (1/4 + 1/8) = 7/8, (1/2 + 1/4) + 1/8 = 7/8; E. 3 x (2 x 5) = 30, (3 x 2) x 5 = 30

**Page 56**
A. 4 x (2 + 3) = (4 x 2) + (4 x 3); B. 3 x (4 + 5) = (3 x 4) + (3 x 5); C. 6 x (2 + 4) = (6 x 2) + (6 x 4); D. 2 x (5 + 2) = (2 x 5) + (2 x 2)

**Page 57**
a = 10; b = 13; c = 6; d = 4; e = 20; f = 11; g = 3.6; h = 5; i = 11.8; j = 2.9; k = 15; l = 6.4; m = 68; n = 12

**Page 58**
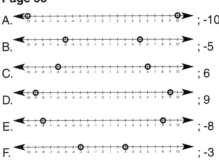

A. ; -10
B. ; -5
C. ; 6
D. ; 9
E. ; -8
F. ; -3

**Page 59**
A. <, >, <, >, >; B. >, =, >, >, <; C. <, <, >, =, <; D. >, >, <, >, <; The bolded temperature should be circled. E. -30°F, **-10°F**; F. **10°F**, -10°F; G. 30°F, **40°F**; H. -40°F, **-25°F**

**Page 60**
A. 4; B. 5; C. -3; Check students' number lines. D. 5; E. -7; F. 7

**Page 61**
A. 1, 1, -11, 9; B. -9, -1, 3, -2; C. 14, 5, 1, -7; D. 3, 1, -4, 3; E. -5, 9, -2, 7; F. -5 + 7 = 2; G. 4 + -10 = -6

**Page 62**
A. 12, -6, 4, -2; B. 13, 13, 4, 4; C. -4, 18, 2, 10; D. 14, -1, -4, 11; E. -12, 10, 8, 4; F. -13, -6, -12, 17

**Page 63**
A. 20, 19; B. 10, 6; C. 13, 10; D. 36, 4; E. 2, 13; F. 15, 5; G. 25, 20; H. 30, 21; I. 1, 5; J. 21, 6; K. 14, 11; L. 6, 16

**Page 64**
A. three hundred forty-five thousand, one hundred twenty-three; B. 20; C. 16; D. 0.4; E. 30%; F. 10; G. 15; H. 1/2; I. 2 2/3; J. $16; K. 10,740; L. 19.164; M. 3.6; N. 11,086; O. 456

**Page 65**
P. 4 x 3 = 12; Q. 16, 20, 24; R. n = 7.1; S. <; T. -12; U. 13; V. 18; W. 19; X. It allows you to visualize the vector addition. Answers will vary.; Y. Answers will vary.

**Page 66**
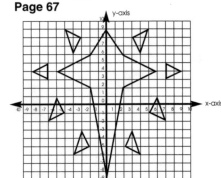

**Page 67**

**Page 68**
A. 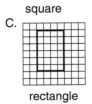 B.

square    trapezoid

C. 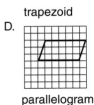 D.

rectangle    parallelogram

E.  F.

parallelogram    rhombus

**Page 69**
A. square    B. rectangle
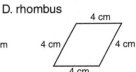
3 cm    5 cm

C. trapezoid    D. rhombus
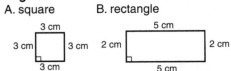

E. triangle    F. parallelogram
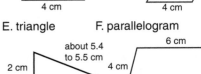
about 5.4 to 5.5 cm

**Page 70**
A. rectangular prism, 6, 12, 8; B. triangular prism, 5, 9, 6; C. cube, 6, 12, 8; D. hexagonal prism, 8, 18, 12; E. pentagonal prism, 7, 15, 10

**Page 71**
A. triangular pyramid, 4, 6, 4; B. octagonal pyramid, 9, 16, 9; C. rectangular pyramid, 5, 8, 5; D. pentagonal pyramid, 6, 10, 6; E. triangular pyramid, 7, 6, 4